CHALLENGE ACCEPTED

CHALLENGE ACCEPTED

50 ADVENTURES TO MAKE MIDDLE SCHOOL AWESOME

CHRIS BALME

zerocirclepress

FOR ABIGAIL

TABLE OF CONTENTS

Introduction 9

50 Challenges

1. Cook a Glorious Meal 13
2. Grow Your Own Food 17
3. Begin a Journal. 21
4. Build a Book Safe 25
5. Be Randomly Kind 29
6. Make a Vision Board. 33
7. Read the World 37
8. Pen Your Appreciation 41
9. Open a Bank Account 45
10. Attend a Local Festival 49
11. Become a Citizen Scientist 53
12. Make an Unexpected Friend 57
13. Be a Stealth Artist 61
14. Join the Global Treasure Hunt 65
15. Try a New Holiday 69
16. Find Awe in Nature. 73
17. Try Yarn Bombing. 77
18. Organize a Yard Sale. 81
19. Connect with an Ancestor 85

TABLE OF CONTENTS

20 Travel Independently 89

21 Become a Sitter 93

22 Share What You Know 97

23 Speak Your Neighbor's Language 101

24 Explore an Unfamiliar Religion. 105

25 Design the Ultimate Test. 109

26 Create a Time Capsule 113

27 Sleep Like a Champion 117

28 Build Something from Scratch 121

29 Discover Wisdom from an Elder. 125

30 Publish Your Work 129

31 Forgive Someone 133

32 Find a Mentor 137

33 Plot a Travel Adventure. 141

34 Talk on the Bright Side 145

35 Train Your Brain 149

36 Level Up Your Habits 153

37 Walk into the Unknown 157

38 Sleep under the Stars 161

39 Stick Out in a Group 165

40 Become an Apprentice 169

41 Ask for Honest Feedback 173

42 Find Shelter in Emotional Storms 177

43 Propose a Better Rule. 181

44 Start a Microbusiness 185

45 Stand Up for Someone 189

46 Heal a Broken Bond 193

47 Turn Cash into Change 197

48 Rescue an Animal 201

49 Be Your Own Boss 205

50 Create Your Own Challenge 209

Note to Parents & Teachers 215

Acknowledgments 219

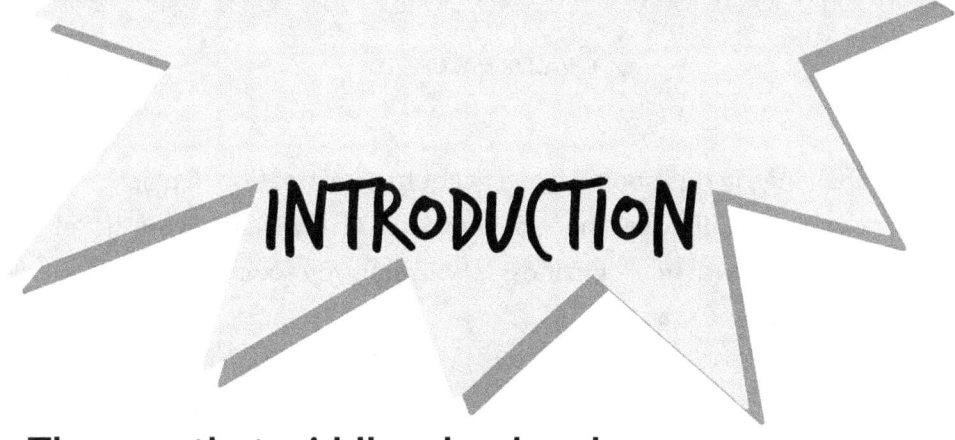

INTRODUCTION

They say that middle school sucks.

It's easy to see why. Middle school can mean loads more homework, intense social drama, and not much choice over how you spend your time.

But that doesn't have to be your story.

You don't have to just drag yourself through middle school. Surprising as it sounds, the middle school years are actually meant to be *magical*.

Did you know that during these years your brain grows faster than it ever will again in your life? In other words, you are getting dramatically smarter every single day. You can feel this, right? But sometimes the rest of the world forgets.

And did you know that for most of history, middle-school-aged kids had a *lot* more freedom? Before modern-day school was invented, middle schoolers were treated like younger adults—trying out real jobs, making real choices, and taking on real responsibilities. That might sound surprising, especially if your middle school experience isn't anything like that.

But that can change. And that's where this book comes in.

In the pages ahead, you'll find 50 challenges designed for middle schoolers. Some might seem crazy. Others are just plain fun. A few might seem impossible (at least according to adults).

Each challenge in this book is like a ticket to a destination. A place where you might discover more of what you can do. Maybe your ticket is starting your own microbusiness, publishing your own book, or sleeping under the stars.

You don't have to try every challenge. Just enough to discover more of what you can do. And you don't have to do them in order. You can follow your heart, choose what looks interesting, or just randomly pick one.

One tip: some of these challenges will seem easy to you. *Skip those ones.* If one makes you a little nervous, that's a sign that it might be worth doing.

And if adults seem shocked by some of these? That's normal. They're just surprised—or confused. Most adults underestimate middle schoolers. It's not really their fault. They were underestimated at this age too.

The truth is, you can do anything.

You can go anywhere.

You can be anyone.

This time in life is meant to be awesome. A year in middle school is like 10 years of growth for an adult. Growing that fast is an epic adventure. What if life could be more like an adventure?

And not just for yourself, but with friends?

It can be. It should be!

This book is your invitation to that awesome adventure.

—CHRIS

1

COOK A GLORIOUS MEAL

Do you love food?

Welcome to the club. We humans love to eat. But here's a secret: food you make yourself *tastes better*.

Why would that be? Well for one, you get to make it exactly how you like it. Plus, when you make it with or for other people, it's one of the most fun ways to spend time together. You can put some music on, let yourself get a little messy, and create something amazing.

Here's another secret: *food is the best gift.* Can you imagine sitting down to a beautiful meal that *you* made and seeing smiles spread across your family's or friends' faces? When you've made something delicious with your own two hands, and someone else gets to enjoy it, it's one of the best things you can do for another person.

GETTING STARTED

1 Start small. If you haven't cooked much yet, you may want to practice with a few small dishes. Easier ones like rice, pasta, or salads can help to get you going. If you know some adults who are good cooks, you could ask them for a little help to start.

2 Create a menu. Once you have some practice, you could create a menu for a meal you'd like to serve. Maybe you have some family recipes, personal favorites, or a cookbook around your home. Libraries are great places to find ideas too. Once you have the menu and recipes, you can make a list of all the ingredients you need.

3 Go shopping. Some of those ingredients might be sitting around your kitchen already. For everything else, it's time to go shopping. You may need to get permission and some spending money from your family if possible. You could even go to the store and do all the shopping on your own.

4 Practice. Chances are, the people who usually make you food have done that about a thousand times for all your favorite dishes, so if it looks easy, it's just because they've practiced so much. You don't have to make your menu a thousand times, but it would be a good idea to make each dish at least once before the big meal.

5 **Show time.** When would you like to make your family or friends a meal? Once you have a date, you can make it a special occasion if you want. You could put on some music, throw a tablecloth on the table, and even photograph your creations. It's not going to be perfect, and that's OK! You could call it a *test kitchen*. This is just the first of many meals you'll get to offer in your lifetime.

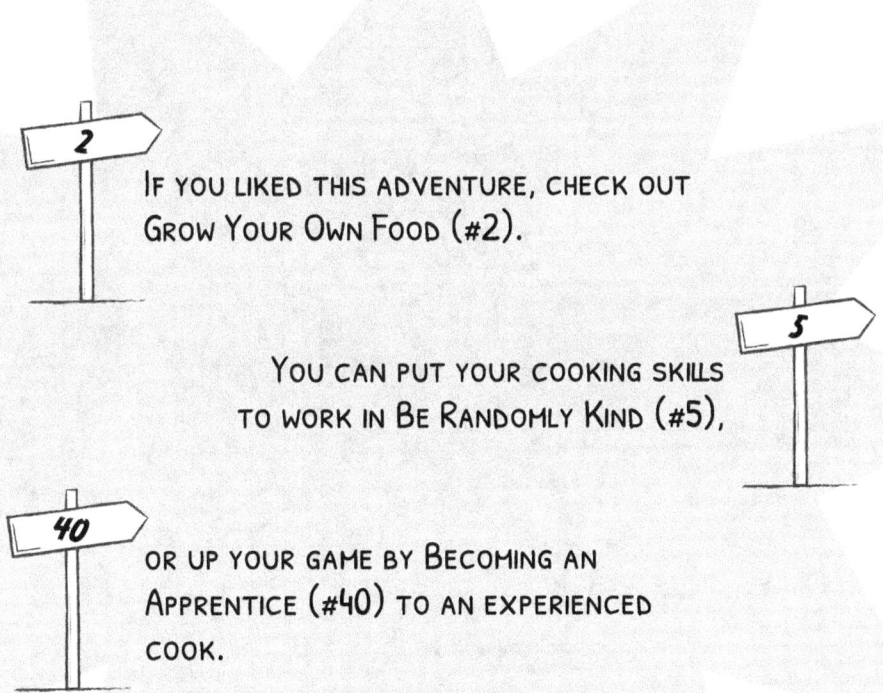

2 IF YOU LIKED THIS ADVENTURE, CHECK OUT GROW YOUR OWN FOOD (#2).

YOU CAN PUT YOUR COOKING SKILLS TO WORK IN BE RANDOMLY KIND (#5), **5**

40 OR UP YOUR GAME BY BECOMING AN APPRENTICE (#40) TO AN EXPERIENCED COOK.

2

GROW YOUR OWN FOOD

Amazing things happen around us every day. A tiny seed grows into a plant, and we eat that plant or what it creates. Then that tomato, carrot, or lettuce leaf actually becomes *you*. What?!

It's hard to believe that every single cell in your body, every bone and every muscle, every bit of your brain was once a piece of food. But it's true. Your body breaks down that sandwich or bowl of pasta into smaller parts and reassembles it into arms and legs. This might be too strange to believe if it weren't part of our everyday life.

When you grow your own food, you start to understand the mystery of how this all works. You see the beginning when the plant is a tiny seed or seedling. You get to nurture it as it grows *and* enjoy the delicious results. And there's no question that food tastes *so much better* when you grow it yourself.

GETTING STARTED

1. ***Where* can you grow?** Do you have space in a backyard, on a porch, or in a community garden? If not outdoors, is there space in your home to grow an indoor plant?

2. ***What* can you grow?** Every plant has its preferences, like how much sun it likes, what kind of soil it needs, and when in the year it grows best. To figure out which plants might work for your situation, you could ask a friend or family member who is good with plants, or visit a gardening store to get some advice.

3. **Making a choice.** Now that you know your options, you can choose a plant to grow. If you're not sure what to choose, you might want to grow one that can become an ingredient in one of your favorite meals.

4. **Gathering supplies.** Once you know what you want to grow and where, you can gather the supplies to make it happen. That probably means seeds or seedlings, a small shovel, and possibly

a pot and some good soil. You don't necessarily have to buy all of these — friends or family might have extras around.

5 **Plant parent mode.** In your research, you probably learned how much water, sun, and space your plant needs, and maybe any nutrients you need to add to the soil. All of that knowledge, plus a little time and love, will make you an awesome plant parent.

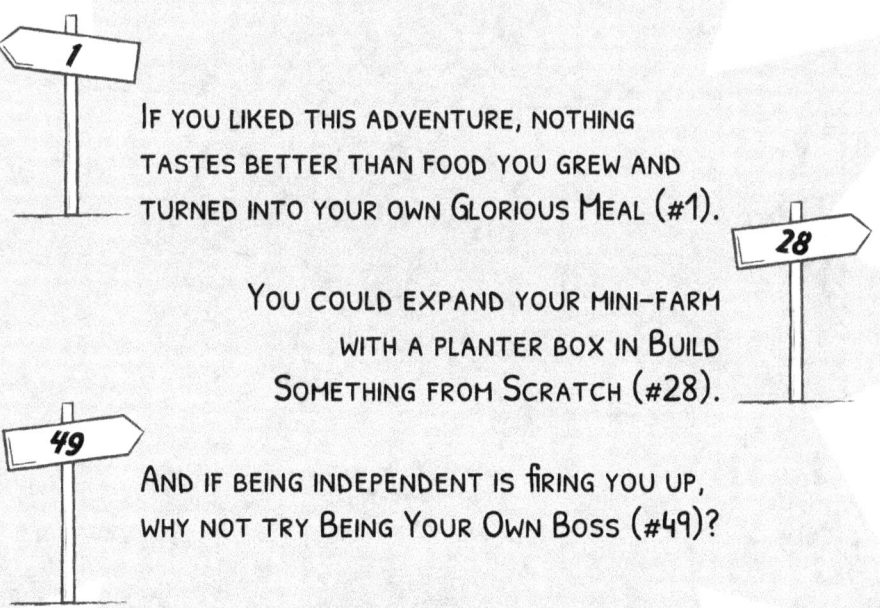

1

IF YOU LIKED THIS ADVENTURE, NOTHING TASTES BETTER THAN FOOD YOU GREW AND TURNED INTO YOUR OWN GLORIOUS MEAL (#1).

28

YOU COULD EXPAND YOUR MINI-FARM WITH A PLANTER BOX IN BUILD SOMETHING FROM SCRATCH (#28).

49

AND IF BEING INDEPENDENT IS FIRING YOU UP, WHY NOT TRY BEING YOUR OWN BOSS (#49)?

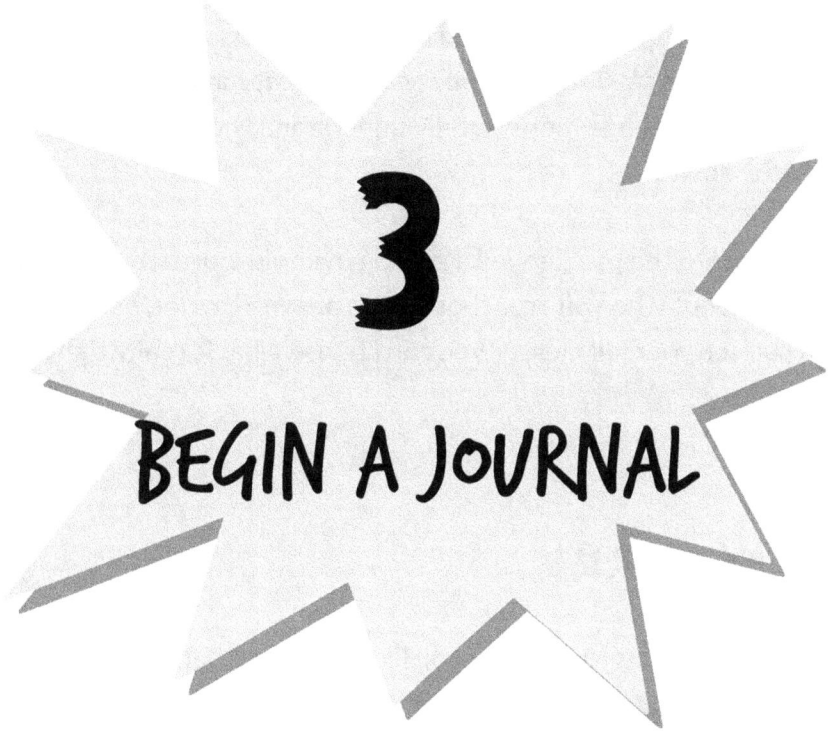

3
BEGIN A JOURNAL

What if you could have a best friend you could always trust? Someone with a totally open mind, ready to hear whatever you're thinking about or feeling?

There is a name for this kind of best friend: *a journal*. And for as long as humans have known how to write, people have kept journals. Most of us need a space like that sometimes — where we can pour out thoughts and feelings, step back and look at them, and see the bigger picture of our lives.

But there's something even more quirky—something seriously strange—that journals offer. In a journal, you can speak directly to your future self. Journals are a *space outside of time.* It can be surprisingly comforting to write down questions for your future self, knowing that by then, everything's been figured out. *Did that person like me back? What was high school like? How did I figure out that conflict?* Your future self, reading those questions, totally understands how you felt *and* also knows the answers.

You can go into the past as well. Reading over old journal entries gives you clues about who you are. Those clues are worth a lot, because when you see yourself clearly, you can choose what is really right for you.

GETTING STARTED

1 **Where will you journal?** If you like writing by hand, you could get yourself a good-quality notebook. Or you can write on a computer or tablet, or even by recording voice notes. Want it to be more social? You could try journaling by exchanging letters with a friend, or by posting private blog entries for select friends to read.

2 **How will you journal?** Some people like the feeling of an open page, and they write whatever pops into their head. Others really like structure. You could give yourself a prompt, like noticing one beautiful thing about the day. Others like the *rose, thorn, and bud* approach — the rose is the best part of your day, the thorn is the hardest, and the bud is something you're interested in or wondering about.

3 **Make it a habit.** Journaling gets really good when you have a habit of doing it regularly, and like all habits, we need little reminders. For example, maybe you could start a routine of writing at least one line in your journal before you go to bed. When you journal in the same place, at roughly the same time, a habit will grow more easily.

4

IF YOU LIKED THIS ADVENTURE, YOU MIGHT WANT TO BUILD A BOOK SAFE (#4) TO KEEP YOUR JOURNAL SAFE FROM PRYING EYES.

26

OR BETTER YET, PUT IT IN A TIME CAPSULE (#26) FOR FUTURE YOU TO ENJOY.

8

AND IF WRITING IS THE PART YOU LOVE, YOU MIGHT BE READY TO PEN YOUR APPRECIATION (#8).

4

BUILD A BOOK SAFE

It's human nature to want to hide our most precious things. And it's just *smart* to hide them in plain sight, where no one would even think to look for them.

There's a secret way that many people have found to do this: you can carve out the inside of a book and turn it into a safe.

It's not too hard to do, and once your work is complete, no one will know that one of those regular-looking books on your shelf is actually a secret compartment for your most valuable belongings. A book safe is a great place to keep precious objects safe from anyone else's eyes.

GETTING STARTED

1 **Gather your supplies.** You'll need a book—a nice thick book with a hard cover, and if possible, one that would have been thrown away otherwise. You'll also need a craft knife and ruler, pencil, and if you want to make it *really* solid, a paintbrush and some white glue or Mod Podge.

2 **Secretly go into action.** You'll want to open the book about 50 pages in. Then, using your ruler and pencil on the top page on the right side of the book, draw a rectangle. The edges of the rectangle should be about one inch from all sides of the page. This will become your safe.

3 **Slice and glue.** Once you have your rectangle marked out, you can carefully use the craft knife to cut into the book. Depending on how thick the paper is, you may want to slice 10-20 pages at a time. Keep going until you get almost to the back cover. Then you can use the paintbrush and some glue or Mod Podge to cover the inside edges of your safe, sealing them closed.

4 **Last touches.** It helps to let the book dry overnight. Your best bet is to close it and put something heavy on top — like a stack of other books—so that it dries without warping the pages. Then your safe is ready to be tucked into the bookcase, hiding in plain sight!

26

IF YOU LIKED THIS ADVENTURE, YOU COULD HIDE MORE TREASURES WITH A TIME CAPSULE (#26),

14

OR SWITCH IT UP AND TRY FINDING SOME WITH A GLOBAL TREASURE HUNT (#14).

17

IF CRAFTING IS YOUR THING, HOW ABOUT YARN BOMBING (#17)?

5

BE RANDOMLY KIND

What if you could make someone's whole day better by slipping a note into their backpack, telling them something you appreciate about them? Or volunteer to do the dishes at home so your parents can take a break? What about surprising your best friend with their favorite drink after school—or helping the new kid find their way to class?

Random acts of kindness can make people *surprisingly* happy. You might not even believe how much of an impact these make until you try. Sometimes the smallest things—like sitting with someone who is alone or sharing your favorite snack—end up meaning the most.

The best part may be how it inspires other people to be kinder too. When someone feels touched by kindness, they're more likely to pass it along and be kind to someone else. Enough kind people might not make math homework go away, but they will definitely make life better.

GETTING STARTED

1 **Choices, choices.** What random act of kindness appeals to you? You could think of one person and imagine what would make them smile, like making them a cup of tea, letting them go in front of you in line, or offering to help them shovel snow or rake their lawn. Or think about something *you* enjoy, like baking cupcakes, and who might love to receive them. Simply giving someone a genuine compliment counts. Your act of kindness doesn't even have to be for someone in particular —you could donate used books to the library or pick up some garbage on the sidewalk.

2 **Don't overthink it!** It can be fun to start with a simple and easy one, and then once you're inspired go for bigger acts of kindness later.

3 **Keep rolling.** What if you made this a part of your day and did a random act of kindness daily for a week? Or more? You might start to notice that other people are copying you—in the best way.

4 **Bonus challenge.** What if you tried doing some of these acts of kindness *secretly*? Like leaving that perfect after-school treat for your friend without a note. Or when you're in line to get a snack somewhere, tell the cashier you'll pay for the next person's order. This can make an even bigger impression on people!

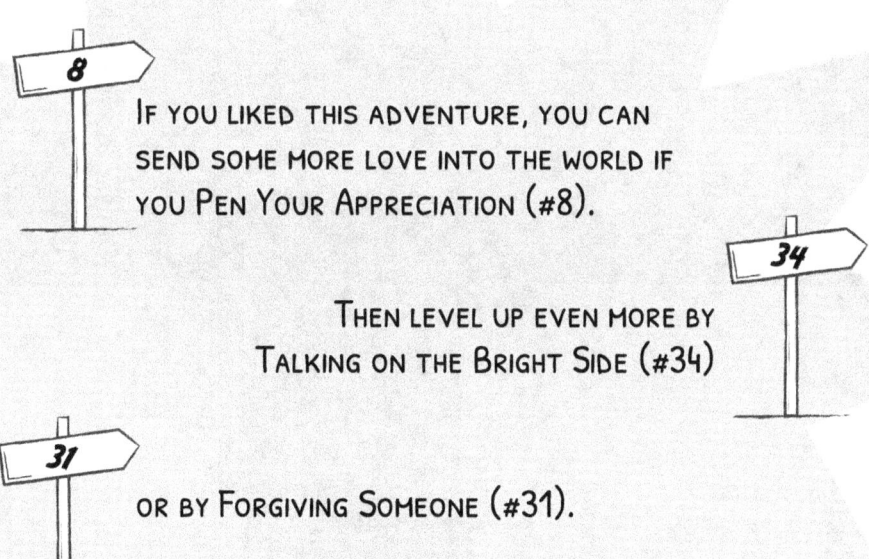

8

IF YOU LIKED THIS ADVENTURE, YOU CAN SEND SOME MORE LOVE INTO THE WORLD IF YOU PEN YOUR APPRECIATION (#8).

34

THEN LEVEL UP EVEN MORE BY TALKING ON THE BRIGHT SIDE (#34)

31

OR BY FORGIVING SOMEONE (#31).

6

MAKE A VISION BOARD

Can you imagine your dream life?

We all have ideas for what that looks like. Maybe it's about being surrounded by good friends. Traveling to a foreign country. Becoming a fantastic soccer player. Or leveling up your coding skills. It feels great to know what you're aiming for.

But there's a catch: life is *really* good at distracting us. It's easy to forget about even our most important goals. Today it's too much homework, tomorrow it's drama at school, and all of a sudden that big dream has been forgotten.

That's where the Vision Board comes in. It's a place where you put images and words that represent your most important goals. It can be on paper or online. It's a totally personalized and beautiful reminder of what matters to you.

When you have your goals in mind, you're more likely to find ways to achieve them. Vision Boards help you stay true to yourself. Maybe it's time to make one!

GETTING STARTED

1 **On paper or online?** If you'd like to create one on paper, it helps to have a big sheet to work with, like poster paper. If designing one online sounds right, tools like Google Slides, Miro, or Canva will give you plenty of space to fill with images and words.

2 **Which images?** It helps to find 10-20 images that mean something to you. These could be photos of loved ones, of yourself in different moments, or images you find online or in magazines—anything that connects to your dreams or values.

3 **Which categories?** Looking at the images you chose, what do you think they represent? For example, some might represent the value of close friendship or a sport you love. Here are some other categories to consider: a new habit or skill you'd like to build, a person or quote who inspires you, something good you could do for the world, an adventure you want to go on, or a person or group who really matters to you.

4 **Putting it all together.** Once you have categories and images, you can put them together in a beautiful way, in your own style. Some people like to choose five to ten images and have a caption or a few words next to each. For example, if one goal is to become a good swimmer, you could write that down next to an image of a pool. You can add as much decoration as you like.

5 **Put it somewhere memorable.** The magic of Vision Boards is that they draw your attention to what really matters to you. It helps to put yours where you can see it regularly, like on your bedroom door, next to where you do your homework, or as your device's background.

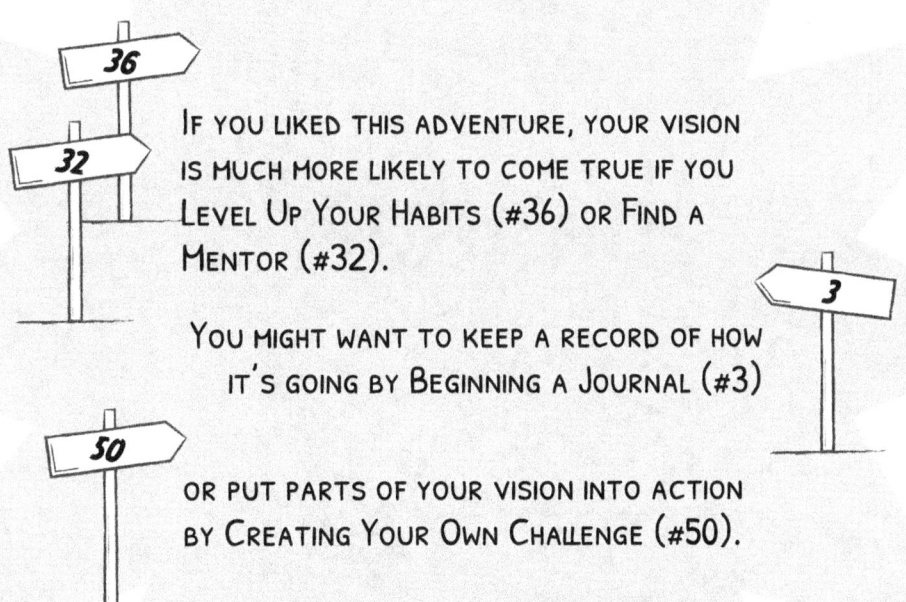

36
32

IF YOU LIKED THIS ADVENTURE, YOUR VISION IS MUCH MORE LIKELY TO COME TRUE IF YOU LEVEL UP YOUR HABITS (#36) OR FIND A MENTOR (#32).

3

YOU MIGHT WANT TO KEEP A RECORD OF HOW IT'S GOING BY BEGINNING A JOURNAL (#3)

50

OR PUT PARTS OF YOUR VISION INTO ACTION BY CREATING YOUR OWN CHALLENGE (#50).

7

READ THE WORLD

It would be weird if someone was watching you all the time, right? Well, I hate to say it, but this is close to what most websites and apps do.

They keep a record of every single thing you watch, read, or react to. It may or may not be evil, but it does mean one thing for sure: they will feed you more of whatever grabs your attention. A *lot* more.

Click on a post about sports? You'll get dozens more. At first, it might seem cool—like the internet *knows* you. But here's the downside: it keeps giving you more of the same while quietly hiding other things that might interest you, too.

The problem with that is there's a lot more of the world to see. You might be missing some of the best parts of it.

So here's one antidote. What if you picked up an old-fashioned newspaper — a real printed copy—and actually read the whole thing? Yes, it sounds crazy. Yes, some of it will be boring. But you'll discover something too. Reading a newspaper is like discovering you've been living in a house but have only been allowed into a few rooms, and now you can look into all the rest. What can you find?

GETTING STARTED

1 **Which newspaper?** There are a *lot* out there. A good starting point would be to choose one of the major daily newspapers. In the US, the five biggest are *The New York Times*, *The Wall Street Journal*, *The Washington Post*, *USA Today*, and *The Los Angeles Times*. Your local grocery or convenience store probably has one or more of them, or you can read one for free at the library.

2 **Every source has bias.** Even the best newspapers in the world are giving you more than the facts — they also mix in some opinions and have their own way of seeing the world. If you find a topic that really interests you, it's a good idea to read about it in different news sources, so you can find out more and make up your own mind about it.

3 **Read away!** Once you have your newspaper in mind, all you have to do is find a comfortable spot and read it from cover to cover. What was most interesting? What did you expect to be boring but actually surprised you?

26

IF YOU LIKED THIS ADVENTURE, YOU COULD TAKE SOME PARTS OF THAT NEWSPAPER AND USE IT TO START AN AWESOME TIME CAPSULE (#26).

19

OR IF IT HAS YOU CURIOUS ABOUT HOW THE WORLD CAME TO BE THIS WAY, YOU MIGHT TRY TO CONNECT WITH AN ANCESTOR (#19).

8
PEN YOUR APPRECIATION

Gratitude is, well, weird. Weird because saying you're grateful doesn't sound like it would make much of a difference, but somehow, it does. Research has shown that writing even a few notes of gratitude can make you feel happier *for weeks*. How could that possibly be?

It turns out our brains tend to focus more on problems than on positives. It's normal to worry and be anxious about all kinds of things.

But if we aren't careful, we can forget to focus on the good stuff. That's where gratitude comes in. It helps you see *all* of your life, not just the annoying parts.

Gratitude points your brain toward the people, moments, and things that make you happier. So it isn't just about writing that one note— gratitude reminds you of all the good things that exist around you.

Oh, and there's one other side effect —maybe the most obvious one! When you share your gratitude with someone, you're going to make them *much* happier. It's kind of perfect. Weirdly perfect.

GETTING STARTED

1 **Notice.** You can start by noticing the good things happening around you—even the tiny ones. Like the fact that you're reading this book in a comfortable room or safe space. Or that you had food earlier today that someone made or bought for you. Or that your friend cares about you and shows it.

2 **Choose.** Of all those good things you can notice, is there one person who comes to mind that you feel grateful for? This could be a teacher, a friend, a family member, or even someone you don't know directly, like someone famous who inspires you.

3 **Write.** Gratitude is even more powerful when you find a way to express it. And nothing beats a hand-written note. It pretty much guarantees you will make someone's day. It doesn't have to be long — it could be as simple as *I just wanted to say that I am grateful for you* — or you could add a bit more detail about what they did or how it makes you feel.

4 **Deliver.** If you can hand it to them, beautiful. If that feels awkward, it's OK to leave it for them somewhere. Depending on who it is, you could send it in the mail.

5 **Bonus challenge.** Why stop with one? The more you do this, the stronger your gratitude muscle will be.

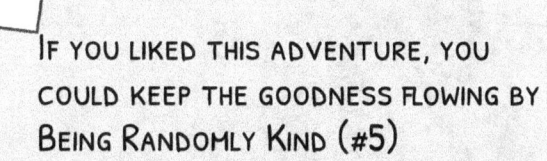

5

IF YOU LIKED THIS ADVENTURE, YOU COULD KEEP THE GOODNESS FLOWING BY BEING RANDOMLY KIND (#5)

45

OR EVEN PUT IT MORE INTO ACTION BY STANDING UP FOR SOMEONE (#45).

34

AND WHY NOT BRING SOME OF THAT GOODNESS INTO YOUR OWN WORLD BY TALKING ON THE BRIGHT SIDE (#34)?

9

OPEN A BANK ACCOUNT

If you haven't opened a bank account yet, you might be surprised to learn that banks actually *pay you* for the privilege of keeping your money safe. It's kind of crazy, but in a good way.

So when you open a bank account, not only is your money safe, but it also starts to grow. Your money starts to make more money.

You can also get checks and a debit card. Checks are slips of paper that tell the bank to send your money to someone else. A debit card does the same thing but faster—it sends an electronic message to take money straight from your account when you buy something.

Once you have a bank account, you can use money for adventures now *and* save for bigger ones later. And when you save enough, you can even put your money in special accounts like CDs (certificates of deposit) or high-yield savings accounts, where your money grows even faster.

GETTING STARTED

1 **Open a joint bank account.** Most banks have two kinds of accounts. *Checking accounts* are for spending money regularly, and *savings accounts* hold money for a long time. You may want to start with a checking account first. To do that, you'll need a parent or guardian to open it with you as a *joint account*, which just means that both your name and their name are on the paperwork. Watch out for any monthly fees on the account—banks should not charge you anything for this.

2 **Make your first deposit.** If you have some cash saved at home, this is your chance to put it safely in the bank. Or you could earn money with some small jobs, maybe from your family or neighbors. A deposit just means bringing this money to the bank so that they can keep it safely in your account.

3 **Get your checkbook and debit card.** You'll receive a checkbook and possibly a debit card with your account. It's a good idea to put these somewhere safe, but you don't have to hide them away — you can use them to spend your money when you need to.

4 **Create a savings account next.** With a savings account, the bank will keep your money safe *and* pay you for letting it do that. The amount they pay you is weirdly called *interest*, and measured by a percentage. If the interest is 5%, that means that if you put in $100, the bank will pay 5% of that, or $5, for every year your money is there. This may not sound like much, but over time it really adds up.

5 **This is only the beginning.** Small choices can make a big difference. There is something called *compound interest*, which means that the interest the bank pays you starts adding up faster and faster over time. If you're money-smart in middle school, you're on track to making money work for you, not the other way around.

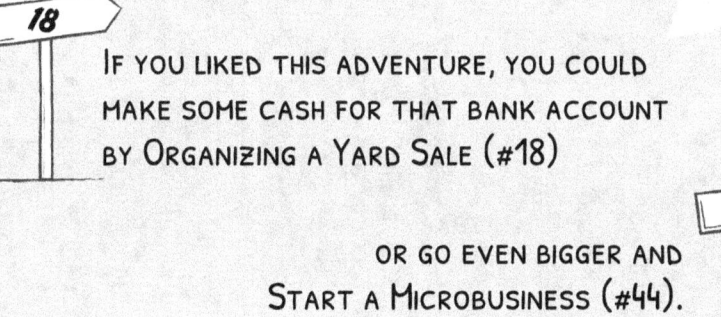

18

IF YOU LIKED THIS ADVENTURE, YOU COULD MAKE SOME CASH FOR THAT BANK ACCOUNT BY ORGANIZING A YARD SALE (#18)

44

OR GO EVEN BIGGER AND START A MICROBUSINESS (#44).

4

IF YOU WANT TO KEEP SOME OF YOUR CASH ON HAND, WHY NOT BUILD A BOOK SAFE (#4)?

10

ATTEND A LOCAL FESTIVAL

Yes, just what you've been waiting for — a cheese festival. Hundreds of kinds are available, including the smelliest ones. Or maybe you're more interested in a festival of tacos. We're talking dozens of different kinds, from classic crunchy to Korean fusion to ice cream tacos.

There *is* a festival for playing music underwater, for competitive pillow fighting, and a festival for best scarecrow designs. There might be a festival for just about everything.

What happens when you go to one? Well, you're going to be with people who are super excited about that particular topic. And that causes a strange thing to happen. Their enthusiasm is a tiny bit contagious. It might make you more interested in something than you ever thought possible.

You might think there aren't any interesting festivals in your area, but unless you live in the middle of a desert (and even then), you're probably wrong. They're everywhere. And the best part is that you might just discover a new hobby or passion.

GETTING STARTED

1 **Ask the right people.** You could ask a few adults for some festival recommendations, especially anyone who shares your hobbies. For example, you might ask your art teacher about craft festivals or your aunt who loves cars about the best classic car show around.

2 **Check event listings.** Since the people organizing festivals typically want a big crowd, they are always working to get the word out. If you check local event listings, which could be in newspapers, on bulletin boards, online, or in other places, you're likely to find something.

3 **Festival day.** Maybe you've found a festival that sounds amazing, or maybe it just sounds random in a way that makes you curious. Since festivals have lots of people who are really passionate about the topic, chances are you can ask them a question or two and they will be happy to explain what's going on. Before you go, you may want to pack snacks and water, put on some comfy walking shoes, and bring some spending money. After all, there may be things to buy there that you can't find anywhere else.

4 **Bonus challenge.** Festivals are an awesome experience to share. If you can invite friends to join you, chances are you'll have more fun. A year later you might still be talking about that incredible cheese festival you visited.

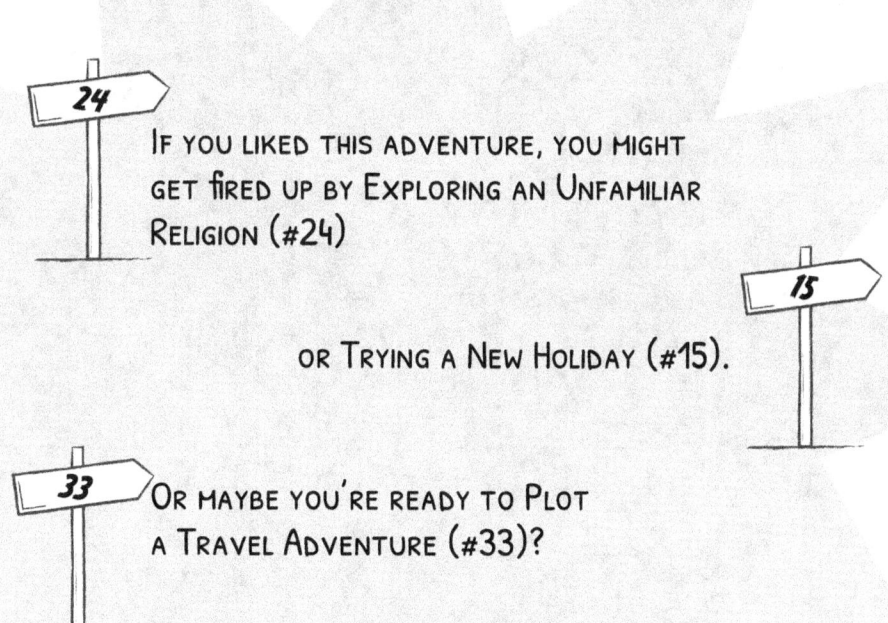

24 IF YOU LIKED THIS ADVENTURE, YOU MIGHT GET fiRED UP BY EXPLORING AN UNFAMILIAR RELIGION (#24)

15 OR TRYING A NEW HOLIDAY (#15).

33 OR MAYBE YOU'RE READY TO PLOT A TRAVEL ADVENTURE (#33)?

BECOME A CITIZEN SCIENTIST

Did you know that all around the world, ordinary people are helping to discover new stars, track rare animals, and solve mysteries about our planet? They're called citizen scientists—people who help with real scientific research projects, right from their own neighborhoods.

Think about the natural world around you. Maybe there's a stream that changes color after it rains, or birds that show up at exactly the same time every year, or plants that grow in unexpected places. Scientists need help observing and recording these kinds of things because there's simply too much happening for them to watch everything themselves.

That's where you come in. From tracking invasive plants or measuring rainfall to photographing cloud patterns or spotting new galaxies on your computer, there are so many ways you can contribute to real scientific discoveries. The best part? You don't need any special equipment or training to begin—just curiosity and attention to detail.

Many of the biggest scientific discoveries came from someone simply paying attention to something unusual in their everyday world. Who knows what you might help discover?

GETTING STARTED

1 **Choose your mission.** What interests you most? Are you fascinated by weather patterns? Love watching birds? Curious about stars? There are citizen science projects for almost every interest. You could help track monarch butterfly migration, measure light pollution in your area, or even help scientists identify new galaxies from space photographs.

2 **Get connected.** Websites like Zooniverse.org or SciStarter.org can help you find projects that match your interests. Maybe you'll count birds at your bird feeder for the Great Backyard Bird Count or use your phone to photograph clouds for NASA's cloud observation project.

3 **Share your discoveries.** The most exciting part of being a citizen scientist is knowing that your observations become part of something bigger. Scientists will use your data, along with information from thousands of other citizen scientists, to understand important changes happening in our world.

4 **Team up.** People who love science love to share ideas, challenge each other, and work together on problems that interest them. If you're enjoying being a citizen scientist, who could work with you? What about your friends, classmates, or even teachers? You could ask for feedback on your observations or come up with ideas for the next experiment together.

27 IF YOU LIKED THIS ADVENTURE, YOU MIGHT BE READY TO APPLY SOME SCIENCE TO YOURSELF AND LEARN HOW TO SLEEP LIKE A CHAMPION (#27).

22 OR YOU MIGHT DECIDE TO TEACH SOME SCIENCE TO A YOUNGER KID BY SHARING WHAT YOU KNOW (#22).

40 THEN TAKE IT TO THE NEXT LEVEL BY BECOMING AN APPRENTICE (#40) TO A PROFESSIONAL SCIENTIST.

12

MAKE AN UNEXPECTED FRIEND

It's easy to *think* you know someone. Like feeling certain that the boy who was a jerk to you in fourth grade will always be a jerk. Or that the girl who is obsessed with sports will never be a friend because you don't care about sports.

We all do it. We make assumptions about other people that we think are true.

The problem is that our assumptions are often just plain wrong. After all, an assumption is just a guess your brain makes. Who knows if it's true until you check?

The worst is when your assumptions are wrong and you don't know it. That person who used to be your enemy might become a good friend — but if you never talk to them again, you would never know. Or that classmate you ignore because they seem weird? They might actually be awesome, but you wouldn't know it either.

Since good friends are one of the best things in life, discovering one would be a sweet reward. But you have to get over your assumptions first. That's where this challenge comes in.

GETTING STARTED

1 **Choosing an unexpected friend.** Is there someone around who you never even tried to be friends with because you were sure it wouldn't go well? We're not talking about anyone mean or terrible here. Just someone you assumed wouldn't have anything in common with you. What if you pretended you had never met them before? Or that you were stuck on a long car ride with them and had to try and connect?

2 **Give it a try.** You can't force a friendship, but you can give it an honest try. You could ask that person a few questions and show you're genuinely interested in who they are. You could look for ways to share an activity together to make it easier to connect.

3 **How to keep going.** It might not work the first time. Or the second or third. But if you keep trying to make unexpected friends, chances are it will work eventually. The beauty of this challenge is that even when it doesn't work out, you get better at talking to all kinds of people. And the more you do it, the easier it gets!

11 IF YOU LIKED THIS ADVENTURE, YOU COULD TRY TO DO AN ACTIVITY WITH YOUR NEW FRIEND, LIKE BECOMING CITIZEN SCIENTISTS (#11) TOGETHER.

39 OR TO BECOME A TRUE MASTER OF AWKWARDNESS, YOU COULD PRACTICE STICKING OUT IN A GROUP (#39).

23 MAYBE YOU JUST ENJOY THE UNFAMILIAR—IN THAT CASE, YOU MIGHT WANT TO TRY AND SPEAK YOUR NEIGHBOR'S LANGUAGE (#23).

13

BE A STEALTH ARTIST

Do you ever feel like there are too many rules? Between school rules, family rules, and all the rules the rest of the world can come up with, it can be a little too much sometimes.

Sometimes it helps to forget about the limits you or others put on yourself. Which is why this challenge is meant to be, well, a little crazy.

This may sound strange, but art is meant to break rules. Some of the most well-known works of art became famous because they pushed boundaries and made not only the artist but everyone seeing it feel more creative.

What if you secretly placed your art somewhere, knowing it will be discovered? Imagine a painting of yours hanging on the wall of a café, or a poem you wrote tucked into the bookcase in your school library. It's weird, but in a good way. If part of you loves making art, and maybe part of you is a ninja and could install it secretly, then this could be the challenge for you.

Your art might get thrown away or it might stay there for years. It might inspire someone to put art in a different spot where you'll never even see it. Who knows what might happen! That's the mystery of this challenge.

GETTING STARTED

1 **What's your style?** If you had the time, what style of art is most fun for you to make? Maybe it's drawing, sculpting, writing, or taking photos.

2 **Why are you making art?** Some people like to make art because it feels good, without any other reason. Other people want a reason or a challenge. If that's you, maybe your reason could be to make someone laugh or inspire them, to tell a story, to show how you're feeling, or to just look beautiful.

3 **Creative time.** When you're ready to begin, you can give yourself some time to make art, in the style and for the reasons that make sense to you (or no reason at all!). It might help to remember that art is not about perfection—whatever you make counts as art.

4 **Find your secret gallery.** Where could someone stumble across your art and smile? What if you taped a poem to the side of a library bookshelf or left a small clay sculpture where it will be noticed? Most people won't get mad at you for leaving a piece of art, especially if you install it in a non-damaging way, like by using painter's tape to stick it to the wall.

5 **Bonus challenge.** For extra fun, you can give your secret art installation a small label or caption to make it look more official.

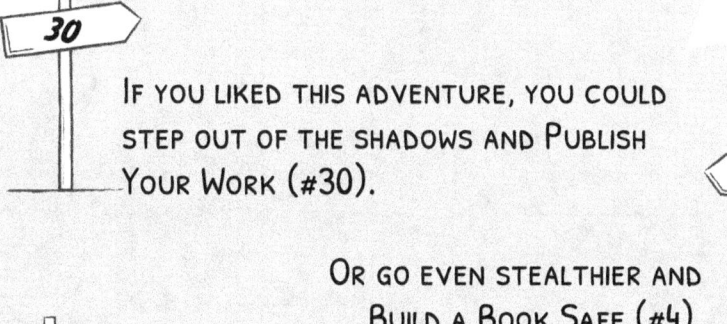

30 IF YOU LIKED THIS ADVENTURE, YOU COULD STEP OUT OF THE SHADOWS AND PUBLISH YOUR WORK (#30).

4 OR GO EVEN STEALTHIER AND BUILD A BOOK SAFE (#4).

14 MAYBE THE MYSTERY OF THIS ADVENTURE IS WHAT SPEAKS TO YOU—IN THAT CASE YOU COULD JOIN THE GLOBAL TREASURE HUNT (#14) OR EVEN BE RANDOMLY KIND (#5).

5

14
JOIN THE GLOBAL TREASURE HUNT

Who *doesn't* like finding treasure? And the more mysterious, the better. So you may be interested to know that more than 3 *million* boxes have been hidden all over the world as part of geocaching —a global treasure hunt that *you* can join.

Each of these secret items has a very specific location. You can find the location details using GPS (which stands for Global Positioning System—the same satellite mapping system that phones use). You then track down a geocache box, open it up, and add a note or sometimes even trade items hidden inside. Once you get the hang of it, you can even add your own geocached treasure boxes and challenge anyone in the world to find them.

GETTING STARTED

1 **Get the gear.** Geocaching is all about using GPS information—also called *coordinates* — to track things down to a specific location. To do this, you'll need either a phone or a handheld GPS device. If you don't own one, you may be able to borrow one.

2 **Find your first cache.** If you go to geocaching.com, you can set up an account and see what might be hidden around you. Before you set off, it might be helpful to take a few key items like water, snacks, a flashlight, and a pen to add your name to the logbook inside most geocaches. Caches use a 5-star rating system for difficulty, so you may want to start with an easier one as you learn.

3 **Treasure-hunting.** The GPS coordinates can get you close—within 30 feet of the treasure. Then it's time to put the device away and start looking. You can ask for hints on the app if needed.

4 **Treasure-finding.** Once you've found one, congratulations! Most caches have a logbook inside, so you can add your name and experience. Some caches have items to trade, like a keychain, coin, or small toy. You can add something and take whatever is there out. To keep the game going, once you're done, you should hide the box in exactly the same spot as before.

5 **Bonus challenge.** If you're really into this, you could try hiding your own geocache treasure. What could you put inside? Where would you hide it? And just like that, the treasure hunt goes on.

33

IF YOU LIKED THIS ADVENTURE, YOU COULD LEVEL UP BY PLOTTING A TRAVEL ADVENTURE (#33) FOR YOUR FRIENDS OR FAMILY.

38

OR IF finDING GEOCACHES OUTDOORS HAS YOU WANTING MORE TIME IN NATURE, HOW ABOUT SLEEPING UNDER THE STARS (#38)?

15
TRY A NEW HOLIDAY

Maybe you look forward to celebrating Lunar New Year with fireworks and festivals. Maybe a Christmas tree loaded with presents is the best part of your year.

We all love a holiday. They give us something to look forward to and a great reason to connect with others.

So if *some* holidays are good, wouldn't *more* holidays be better?

There's a whole world of different cultures out there — including some with awesome holidays you've never heard of. If you learn about them, not only do you get to know the world better, but you get more special days! More reasons to celebrate, and maybe you'll make some new friends and go on new adventures along the way. What could be better?

GETTING STARTED

1 **What's new to you?** You already know some holidays well, so the first step is to go beyond those. The good news is that finding new celebrations is usually easier than you might think. Do you have friends or neighbors who celebrate different holidays?

2 **A few hints.** Listed below are ten holidays from around the world. Chances are you don't celebrate all of these, so maybe some will be new. If one sounds interesting, you could ask a few people for help finding a local place where this holiday is celebrated.

- Diwali (Festival of lights from India)
- Lantern Festival (Celebrated in China and beyond)
- Nowruz (Persian New Year from Iran)
- Sinterklaas (Gift-giving celebration from the Netherlands)
- Hanukkah (Jewish festival of lights)
- Eid al-Fitr (Feast ending Islam's Ramadan holiday)
- Carnival (Colorful pre-Lent celebration in Brazil and other countries)
- Día de los Muertos (Mexico's way of honoring departed loved ones)
- Midsummer (Summer solstice celebration from Sweden)
- Children's Day (Celebration of youth from Japan)

3 **Enjoy!** Since you've picked a holiday you're not familiar with, don't be surprised if you are, well, surprised! After all, that's the point of doing this. Chances are that the holiday you chose has lasted for so long because there is something really special about it. Can you figure out why people love it?

24

IF YOU LIKED THIS ADVENTURE, YOU COULD KEEP THE DISCOVERY GOING BY EXPLORING AN UNFAMILIAR RELIGION (#24).

10

IF IT'S THE PARTY SPIRIT THAT LIGHTS YOU UP, YOU COULD ATTEND A LOCAL FESTIVAL (#10).

16

FIND AWE IN NATURE

Did you ever wonder where the word awesome comes from? Every time you say it, you're talking about *awe* — that feeling of being amazed and filled with wonder.

Turns out, we really need awe in our lives. Otherwise we tend to get stuck in our heads, worrying about other people, homework, and life in general.

Awe is everywhere, but there is one way to find it whenever you need it. *Nature.* One single tree, if you look closely, is like an explosion frozen in time. It's pretty awesome. If you have the chance to look out over the ocean, feeling tiny in comparison, that's awe too. The night sky twinkling with stars, a thunderstorm rolling in with purple clouds, or even a spider web covered in morning dew—they're all invitations to feel amazed.

Awe is like a reset button for our emotions and thoughts. It would be pretty cool to have your own personal reset button. That's what this challenge is all about.

GETTING STARTED

1 **What draws you in?** Is there a particular kind of nature that seems especially beautiful to you and is nearby? Maybe it's being near water, from an ocean to a forest stream, or maybe it's a mountain, forest, or city park. Some people find it by smell, like a certain plant or flower that has an attractive scent.

2 **Start looking.** It's OK if you're not sure what kind of nature appeals to you — that just means it's time to explore. A good way to start is by practicing really *looking*. That sounds weird, but sometimes we get used to looking so quickly that we don't see much. Instead, try following the currents of water in a river. Or looking at the shape of different leaves on a tree. You're building the ability to find awe. You could also try asking some friends or adults for beautiful spots in nature near you. If you put yourself in a few of those places and look around carefully, you'll notice which ones make you feel good.

3 **Make it yours.** Even if you're not totally sure after choosing a place, it's still a good starting point. If you visit it regularly, you might begin to feel connected to it. You might even notice how it changes in different seasons. It becomes *yours* in some strange way. It doesn't have to be far away, and you don't have to climb Mount Everest to feel awe in nature. If you can find a place nearby that creates awe in you, then you have an easy way to reset your mind and feel peaceful and amazed whenever you want.

38

IF YOU LIKED THIS ADVENTURE, WHY STOP AT VISITING NATURE BRIEFLY WHEN YOU COULD SLEEP UNDER THE STARS (#38)?

14

WHILE YOU'RE THERE YOU COULD JOIN THE GLOBAL TREASURE HUNT (#14).

17

OR MAYBE YOU'RE READY TO INFUSE NATURE WITH SOME OF YOUR OWN ARTISTIC SPIRIT BY YARN BOMBING (#17)?

17
TRY YARN BOMBING

What if there were a *friendly* kind of graffiti? One that turns ordinary spaces into works of art, adds color and fun, and actually makes people *smile*?

It turns out there is, and it has a strange name: *yarn bombing*.

Yarn bombing is when you choose an object out in the world, like a tree limb, part of a park bench, or a light pole, and you transform it by wrapping or knitting yarn around it. All of a sudden that boring thing you see every day becomes colorful and playful. There you have it—friendly graffiti.

Yarn bombing done well, with permission, brings a cheerful and artsy spirit to spots that would otherwise be dull. It's a crafty way to give the world some more personality.

GETTING STARTED

1 **Where?** Is there some part of the world around you that could use a little color? If you need some inspiration, search for yarn bombing online and you'll find thousands of examples. Some popular choices are tree trunks, bike racks, fences, light poles, railings, mailboxes, and even garden gnomes.

2 **Get permission.** It would be frustrating to have your yarn creation taken off right away or someone upset at you for putting it there in the first place. So it's always a good idea to find a spot where you can figure out who is in charge and ask their permission. You can always offer to take it down if they don't like it.

3 **Sizing.** You can use a measuring tape or simply a piece of string to figure out how big the object is that you'll be covering, to help you plan your design.

4 **Design time.** Now that you have the spot, permission, and the size, you get to design whatever your mind can imagine and your hands can create. You could make one large piece or many small ones that connect. You could do patchwork, knitting, or try other techniques. You can choose which yarns to use and whether you want to do this solo or invite some crafty friends to join.

5 Installation! When it's time to install, you may want to bring extra yarn, scissors, a needle and hook, some wire to bend certain parts into place, cable ties, and possibly a ladder if needed. Then, you get the chance to yarn-graffiti one corner of the world into something fun and beautiful.

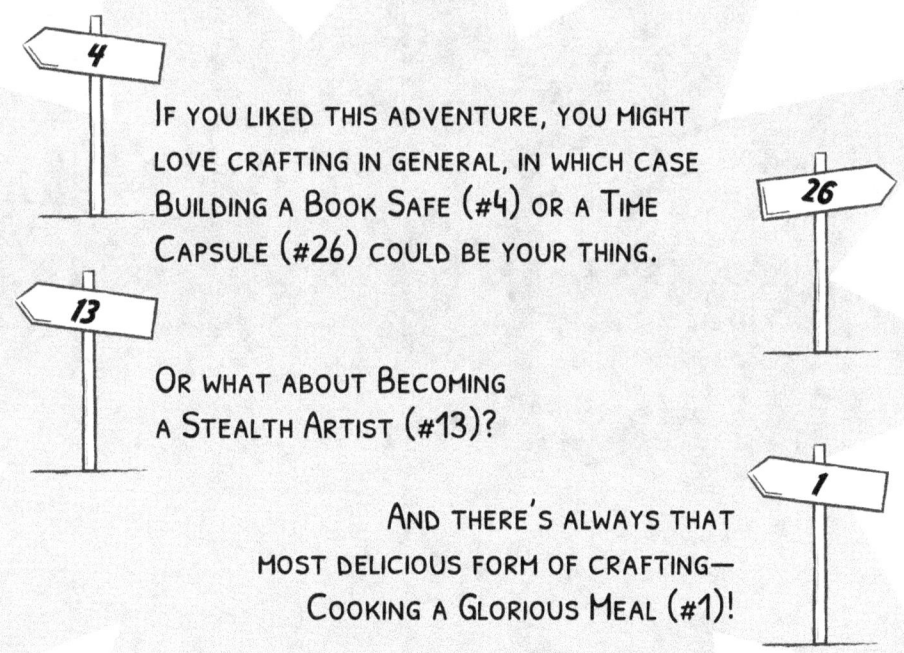

4

IF YOU LIKED THIS ADVENTURE, YOU MIGHT LOVE CRAFTING IN GENERAL, IN WHICH CASE BUILDING A BOOK SAFE (#4) OR A TIME CAPSULE (#26) COULD BE YOUR THING.

26

13

OR WHAT ABOUT BECOMING A STEALTH ARTIST (#13)?

1

AND THERE'S ALWAYS THAT MOST DELICIOUS FORM OF CRAFTING— COOKING A GLORIOUS MEAL (#1)!

18

ORGANIZE A YARD SALE

Everyone has junk at home. Some of us have a *lot* of junk. What if someone else might really want it, and you could free up some space? What if you could even turn that junk into some cash?

This is where a yard sale comes in (and you don't even need a yard to do it). A yard sale just means gathering up items from your home that still have some value (for someone!) and selling them. It's part treasure hunt and part business adventure.

GETTING STARTED

1 **Junk finder.** The first step is to find all the items in your home that no one in your family wants anymore, but would still be useful to someone else. You may want to clean them up a bit to make them more appealing to buyers.

2 **Date, time & place.** Once you have plenty of items and permission from everyone to sell them, when would you like to have the yard sale, and where? Weekends are ideal so more potential customers have time to come. For location, is there a convenient outdoor space, like a sidewalk or driveway? You may need to get permission if you live in a building with other residents.

3 **Who's with you?** Having a friend or family member be there with you is a big help. Even better, if you have any neighbors who want to have a yard sale on the same day, everyone benefits, since more customers will stop by.

4 **Getting the word out.** This part is key—it would be sad to do all the work for a yard sale but have no customers! Simple flyers on telephone poles or bulletin boards are a classic way. If you have any neighborhood groups, you or your family could spread the word that way too.

5 **Selling time!** On sale day, you may want to spread items out so that buyers can see all of them at a glance. You could put little stickers with price tags on your items if you want, or just tell people the price when they ask. Unlike shopping in stores, people may want to haggle with you and ask for discounts, so it helps to have in mind what your lowest price is. Finally, since some buyers may pay with larger bills and need change, it helps to have some one-dollar and five-dollar bills ready along with a handful of change.

6 **Give away the rest.** Chances are, even if your yard sale is a huge success, a few items will be left over. Since you were already planning on getting rid of them, you can just donate these, maybe to a local charity like Goodwill or the Salvation Army. Then, enjoy the extra space and new cash!

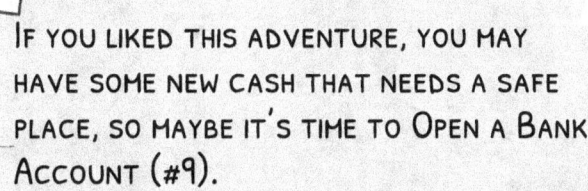

9

IF YOU LIKED THIS ADVENTURE, YOU MAY HAVE SOME NEW CASH THAT NEEDS A SAFE PLACE, SO MAYBE IT'S TIME TO OPEN A BANK ACCOUNT (#9).

47

PERHAPS YOU WANT TO USE THE MONEY YOU MADE FOR OTHERS AND TURN CASH INTO CHANGE (#47).

44

OR PERHAPS YOU FOUND A LOVE OF BUSINESS, IN WHICH CASE IT COULD BE TIME TO LEVEL UP AND START A MICROBUSINESS (#44).

19

CONNECT WITH AN ANCESTOR

So this one is *not* about being able to talk with ghosts (that would be cool and also really creepy). This one is about finding inspiration in that long line of people who all led directly to *you*—your ancestors.

Do you know who your ancestors are? Your great-grandparents or even further back? Is there someone whose story stands out, who makes you think *I wish I could've met them*?

If you're wondering why this even matters, think about a tree. You may see its trunk, branches, and leaves—but are you actually seeing the whole tree? Not even close. If that were all of it, it would fall over easily! There is a huge root system beneath the tree, anchoring it to the ground through storms while providing water and nutrients. You couldn't really understand a tree if you looked at it only from the ground up.

Humans are like this too. What we see—names, personalities, talents—is just the top half. The roots are our family history—the journeys our ancestors took and the stories they passed down. In this challenge, you'll discover more about that family story and the characters in it. As you do, you may start to see yourself as a tree with strong roots holding you steady even in stormy weather. And along the way, you might meet a fascinating character or two who shaped your life without you even knowing it.

GETTING STARTED

1. **A family tree.** You've probably seen or even made one: a giant piece of paper where your name is at one end, and then you work backward in time. Your name, maybe circled or in a box, connects to boxes for each of your parents, then to their parents and siblings, and so on. But this time, the goal isn't just to write down the names of each ancestor. The real goal is to meet someone, at least in your imagination, from your family's past. For each ancestor, see if you can find out what their life was really like. Where did they grow up? What were things like then? What were the turning points in their lives? This challenge is a quest to understand your family and to find someone—from all those characters in the past—who connects with *you*.

2 **A documentary.** Another option is to find a living family member older than your parents—like a grandparent or great-uncle—and discover more about their story. What if you made a mini-documentary about their life? You could film them (or family members related to them) answering a series of questions. You could ask about their proudest moments, their struggles, major life choices they weren't sure about, or the people in their early lives who influenced them. Sometimes people are just waiting for good questions in order to tell their story. You might be amazed by the adventures they've had.

6

IF YOU LIKED THIS ADVENTURE, SOME CLUES FROM YOUR FAMILY STORY COULD HELP YOU MAKE AN AWESOME VISION BOARD (#6).

32

OR IF YOU'RE HUNGRY FOR MORE LEARNING FROM AN OLDER PERSON, MAYBE IT'S TIME TO FIND A MENTOR (#32)?

41

AND IF YOU'RE *REALLY* BOLD, YOU MIGHT DARE TO ASK FOR HONEST FEEDBACK (#41).

20
TRAVEL INDEPENDENTLY

Do you ever feel stuck at home, waiting for people to take you places? Do you ever wish that you could get around more on your own?

If you answered yes, then this challenge might be for you. The world has too much good stuff in it—like friends to see, beautiful nature to explore, or stores where you can shop—to stay put in one spot.

The trick is to learn how to travel safely and help the adults in your life feel confident about you going out on your own. Chances are they want this for you as well, but are a bit nervous about it. Here's how to help them (and you) get comfortable with traveling on your own.

GETTING STARTED

1 **Where can you go?** You may need some advice from adults about what level of independence is safe for your age and region. True, they might tend to underestimate you. But if you show them your abilities step by step, there's a good chance that they will eventually relax and begin to give you more freedom. Can you think of a destination that would let you test your independence? Maybe it's just a *little* farther than you've gone before, like cycling to a friend's house instead of getting a ride, running a local errand for your family, or going to school on your own.

2 **How would you get there?** If you have a phone, you can use a mapping app. If you don't, you can print out or buy a map of the area. If you plan to take a bus or train, you can do a little research in advance to learn the routes, timing, and costs so you're ready. You can always ask family or friends for some advice on the best way to get somewhere.

3 **How are your street smarts?** *Street smarts* means being able to handle tricky situations, like getting lost or noticing if the area you're in feels unsafe. The details depend on where you live, so it may be wise to talk to a few adults about what they would recommend. For example, if you find yourself lost or scared for some reason and you're in a town or city, one good tip is to find a café, library, or convenience store where you could ask an adult to use the phone. It's also a good idea to have at least one phone number memorized so you can contact an adult at any time.

4 **Test run.** If your plan is stretching everyone's comfort zones, you may want to try a test run first. Share your route and plan with your trusted adults. Maybe they'll need to go with you for part or all of your journey the first time. When you show your skills and maturity, you'll help them trust you to do this on your own.

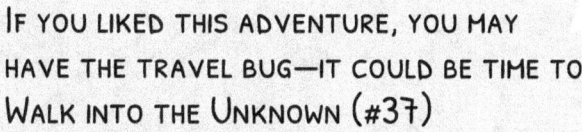

37 IF YOU LIKED THIS ADVENTURE, YOU MAY HAVE THE TRAVEL BUG—IT COULD BE TIME TO WALK INTO THE UNKNOWN (#37)

33 OR PLOT A TRAVEL ADVENTURE (#33) WITH FAMILY OR FRIENDS. THERE'S A WHOLE OTHER WORLD TO EXPLORE INDEPENDENTLY IN THE WILDERNESS TOO,

38 AND IF THAT SPEAKS TO YOU, CHECK OUT SLEEP UNDER THE STARS (#38).

21
BECOME A SITTER

Sometimes the biggest adventures don't require going anywhere. Here's one that might push you out of your comfort zone—but in an awesome way. What if you could become a sitter—and not just any sitter, but a really good one?

It might seem scary if you aren't used to it. Sure, you have to be ready for anything, from a five-year-old getting hurt during playtime to a diaper change if it's a baby. And you can't press pause while watching a little kid to take a break. It's an intense amount of responsibility.

But there are ways to practice the skills you need, and there are some great rewards as a result. You might be surprised how much fun it is to play with a younger kid—someone who doesn't worry about the same things you do. You might even feel pretty close to them after a while. And you'll definitely earn the right to feel proud—you're someone a family trusts with their child.

Last but not least, babysitting is one of the *best* ways to earn money as a middle schooler. Good sitters are always in demand.

GETTING STARTED

1 **Who needs help?** Most parents could use more help, especially when their kids are young. You might want to start by looking at your extended family — do any cousins, aunts, uncles, etc., have kids younger than you? If not there, you could think about friends and their families, people in your neighborhood, or your parents' friends.

2 **Begin as a parent's helper.** Once you've found someone who needs help, you can give yourself an easy start by doing it for free at first while the parent is still at home. This lets you practice without feeling all the responsibility on your shoulders. It also builds trust, as you show the parents that you're reliable and responsible. You may want to come up with a list of questions about topics like food preparation, bedtime routines, or favorite games or books.

3 **Start babysitting.** Once you have some practice, it may be possible to start babysitting regularly, with the family you began with and eventually others too. The more experience you have, the more in demand you will be. You can start to charge for your services, too. You'll be running your own mini-business, proving how responsible you are, and likely having a pretty great time doing it.

22

IF YOU LIKED THIS ADVENTURE, YOUNGER KIDS WILL THINK YOU'RE EVEN COOLER WHEN YOU SHARE WHAT YOU KNOW (#22).

44

AND IF YOU'RE ENJOYING HOW BABYSITTING EARNS YOU SOME MONEY, YOU COULD LEVEL UP BY STARTING A MICROBUSINESS (#44).

32

WHAT IF YOU FLIPPED THE SCRIPT AND FOUND AN OLDER PERSON TO GUIDE YOU BY FINDING A MENTOR (#32)?

22

SHARE WHAT YOU KNOW

It's easy to think about all the things you *don't* know yet. But when you focus on those things, you might forget how far you've come.

For example, you probably aren't jumping up and down every day because you can read, or ride a bike. You're just used to it. You've already learned thousands of skills and perfected so many things. What would it feel like to give yourself some credit for that?

Here's one way to remember that *and* help someone else. What if you taught a younger child something you know? It could be riding a bike or skateboard, balancing on a scooter, juggling, reading, learning multiplication, or a million other things.

You might be surprised how fun it is. Watching them figure out something they couldn't do before is going to feel great. And it may just remind you how much you've already learned.

GETTING STARTED

1 **What do you know?** You know *so* much—it's just a matter of picking where to start. If you think of three categories—academics, sports, and hobbies—what's your best skill in each one? You don't have to be an expert. If you can teach it to someone a few years younger, you're ready.

2 **Who needs help?** A younger kid is going to think you're the coolest person ever. They probably want to learn anything you'd like to teach. But if you can find a specific skill they *really* want to learn, it's even better. Maybe there's a friend's sibling or a neighbor's kid who wants to learn how to read or ride a bike. If you don't know anyone like that, you could tell a few friends and adults about your three best skills and that you'd like to try teaching them to someone younger.

3 **Small steps.** Great teachers break things down into small steps. If you're teaching juggling, that might mean first catching one ball back and forth, then adding a second ball with a simple cross pattern, and finally moving up to three balls. If it's skateboarding, maybe you begin with just standing on the board while holding a fence, then pushing off with one foot, before teaching them to turn. Each small step they accomplish will build up their confidence for your next suggestion.

4 **Patience.** Like any good challenge, there's got to be something that pushes you a bit. With teaching, that challenge might be the sheer amount of patience it requires. Say you're showing someone how to draw anime characters — they might spend an entire session just practicing basic eye shapes. That's okay! Remember how long it took you to get good at this? Small wins add up to big victories, and being patient while someone else learns something you love can make you appreciate your own journey even more.

25

IF YOU LIKED THIS ADVENTURE, YOU MIGHT ENJOY GUIDING OTHERS THROUGH A DIFFERENT KIND OF CHALLENGE BY DESIGNING THE ULTIMATE TEST (#25).

40

AND WHEN YOU'RE READY TO LEARN THE NEXT AWESOME SKILL YOU MIGHT SHARE ONE DAY, NOTHING BEATS BECOMING AN APPRENTICE (#40).

23

SPEAK YOUR NEIGHBOR'S LANGUAGE

Do you *really* know the area where you live? It might seem so familiar, especially if you've lived there a long time. But what if there's more going on around you than you realize?

Take language, for example. Chances are you speak one or two languages. But there are around 7,000 human languages in the world today. It's almost guaranteed that some of those other 6,998 options are spoken around you as well. And each one is like a doorway to a whole world of people.

To open those doors, this challenge is about learning a bit of a new language. After all, we humans are talkers. When you learn a new language, you're really learning how to connect with new people. This challenge will require a bit of detective work and some practice, but the fun of making new connections in your own neighborhood makes it all worthwhile.

GETTING STARTED

1 **Who's out there?** What languages are spoken in your area? If you keep your ears open or ask around, you'll discover them. Maybe closer than you think — it could be friends, neighbors, teachers, through clubs at school, or in restaurants and community centers.

2 **Which language might interest you?** Maybe you know some people you'd love to be able to talk to in their language. Maybe one language just sounds beautiful to you. Maybe you have a favorite kind of food and want to learn the language of the place where it comes from. All of those are good reasons to explore.

3 **Practice time.** Once you've chosen a language, you have a lot of options for how to learn it. You could ask someone if they would teach you a little. Or ask a teacher or friend to recommend some books. You could watch shows in that language. You could study it online through YouTube tutorials or language-learning apps. But the very best practice, once you feel confident, is to use it in real life with someone who speaks it. Even if you can only say a few words, you'll be amazed at how many doors will open.

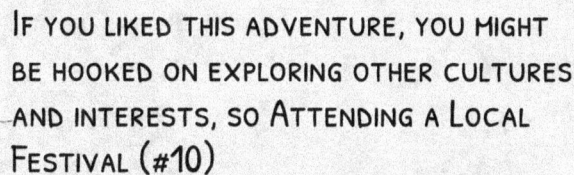

10 IF YOU LIKED THIS ADVENTURE, YOU MIGHT BE HOOKED ON EXPLORING OTHER CULTURES AND INTERESTS, SO ATTENDING A LOCAL FESTIVAL (#10)

24 OR EXPLORING AN UNFAMILIAR RELIGION (#24) COULD LIGHT YOU UP.

39 IF YOU ENJOY THE FEELING OF BEING THE DIFFERENT ONE AS YOU EXPLORE, YOU COULD LEVEL UP IN A BIG WAY BY STICKING OUT IN A GROUP (#39).

24
EXPLORE AN UNFAMILIAR RELIGION

Do you ever ask yourself big questions, like what happens after you die? Or whether there are higher powers? It's only natural to wonder about these things. We humans are a curious bunch.

Throughout history there have been thousands of answers to these questions, found in different religions around the world—from the very biggest ones like Islam or Christianity to smaller ones you might not know about yet.

Each one of these religions has fascinating answers. Each also has beautiful rituals, holidays, places of worship, and more. They're like different planets to visit.

Maybe you already know one religion well, or maybe you don't know any yet. There's no bad way to start. The goal is just to explore. If you keep your mind open and curious, you might pick up some ideas for answers to the biggest questions you've ever asked.

GETTING STARTED

1 **Choose a religion.** If you aren't sure where to start, you could ask family or friends, or check out books or websites that introduce different religions. You might find one that intrigues you.

2 **Find a good source.** While you can learn online, nothing beats hearing directly from someone who practices the religion. A family member, friend, teacher, or local place of worship might help you connect. If you're using the internet, just remember that there is a lot of misinformation out there, so it can help to look for sources run by the religion's official groups.

3 **Question time.** If you get the chance to speak with someone who practices this religion, what would you really like to know? Between your research and your own big questions, you can probably create at least 5-10 good questions. And when you ask them with genuine curiosity, not making anyone feel like their religion is strange in any way, chances are you'll get some interesting answers. For example:

- Did you grow up with this religion?

- If so, what are your childhoowd memories of it? If not, how and when did you find it?

👅 How do you practice your religion now, on an average day or week?

👅 How does your religion help you deal with life's ups and downs?

👅 What are some of the religious teachings you think about most?

4 **Let yourself wonder.** After learning about a different religion, you may want to take some time to think about what surprised or interested you the most. Talking about it with a friend or family member is another great way to make sense of it. Even if questions lead only to more questions (not a bad thing!), along the way you'll learn a lot about how other people see the world.

23

IF YOU LIKED THIS ADVENTURE, YOU COULD EXPLORE UNFAMILIAR LANGUAGES BY SPEAKING YOUR NEIGHBOR'S LANGUAGE (#23)

37

OR UNFAMILIAR LOCALES IF YOU WALK INTO THE UNKNOWN (#37).

7

AND IF UNDERSTANDING RELIGIONS MAKES YOU CURIOUS ABOUT HOW THE WORLD WORKS IN GENERAL, YOU MIGHT BE READY TO READ THE WORLD (#7).

25

DESIGN THE ULTIMATE TEST

What's the best obstacle course you've ever seen?

However good it is, chances are you could make an even better one.

Imagine physical challenges, like leaping over a pool of water or jumping through a chute. Add mental puzzles, like trivia questions, riddles, or naming a mystery song that's playing. How about emotional challenges, like having to do a trust walk while blindfolded?

You could even add last-minute twists, like the challenge of walking backward through the obstacle course while holding a glass of water without spilling, or whatever you can come up with! And an obstacle course offers an awesome excuse to hang out with friends. You could challenge them to set personal records or compete against the clock or each other.

GETTING STARTED

1 **Choose your location.** Your backyard, a local park, a room at home, a friend's house, or a community center—all could be great spots.

2 **Dream up your challenges.** Some people like to map it out on paper. Some just jump right in. It's up to you. As you design it, make sure the course is challenging but physically and emotionally safe for everyone.

3 **More ideas.** In case you want to add more challenges to the mix, here are a few to consider:

- Balance Tasks (like walking along a line of tape without stepping off)

- Puzzles (maybe a riddle to solve before you can move on)

- Estimation (like guessing how tall something is, or how many balls are in a jar)

- Animal Moves (walking like a crab or a frog for a certain section)

- Team Activities (where a challenge can only be solved by teamwork)

- Finding Treasure (with clues left along the way)

- Physical Disadvantage (like doing the course with one arm tied behind your back)

4 Testing time. All great video games go through a testing process first, so why not do the same for your obstacle course? You could invite a friend to build it with you, or be your tester, or add their own ideas if you're open to it. Before testing, you may want to do a quick safety check for things like sharp corners or slippery ground.

2

IF YOU LIKED THIS ADVENTURE, YOUR OWN ULTIMATE TEST MIGHT BE TO GROW YOUR OWN FOOD (#2).

28

OR THE NEXT MOVE MIGHT BE TO GO BIG AND BUILD SOMETHING FROM SCRATCH (#28) WITH A FRIEND.

26

CREATE A TIME CAPSULE

Time is a strange thing. In the middle of your most boring class, it might appear to stand still. But when you're hanging out with friends, it rockets by. Maybe that's why most of us wish we could control it more, so we could slow it down for the good stuff and skip the other parts!

What if there were a way to pause time, to freeze one moment and save it for later?

That's what a time capsule is all about. You get to select a few key items from your everyday life—things that show who you are right now—and place them *outside* of time. Buried in your backyard, or tucked away in your closet in a special box, they'll wait until Future You — maybe even Adult You — one day stumbles upon them. Future You will thank Present-Day You in a big way for saving something from this era of your life. And even Present-Day You might enjoy the chance to pause time for a minute and capture memories of your current adventures.

GETTING STARTED

1. **Time travel packing list.** Human memory is not the greatest, so Future You might have forgotten a lot about this era. What could you include that would remind them? You could make a list, or simply start gathering items.

2. **Personal mementos.** These might include an object you love, a school project you completed, a lock of hair, a photo of you and your friends, a toy you treasure, or even a favorite book.

3. **Items from the world.** You could include something that shows what's happening in the world right now, like a newspaper or magazine, a letter with a date on it, or a ticket stub from a movie, concert, or sports event.

4. **A letter or journal.** You could remind Future You what matters to you right now by listing your close friends, your favorite songs or shows, the books you've read recently, or adventures you've gone on. If you want to guarantee a smile on Future You's face, add a list

of memes and favorite slang phrases that you and your friends use. Feel free to include some questions for Future You as well.

5 **How and where to hide it?** You could put this in a box, label it, seal it up with tape, and put it in some out-of-the-way part of your room or home, or even a relative's home. Or if you have outdoor space, you could go a step further and place it in a metal or plastic container and bury it! It's up to you.

6 **Partner up.** It can be especially fun to do this with a good friend. You could work together on one time capsule, or each make your own, inspiring each other and probably laughing a lot as you choose items to include.

3

IF YOU LIKED THIS ADVENTURE, THERE'S A GOOD CHANCE THAT BEGINNING A JOURNAL (#3) WOULD ALSO BE FUN.

OR SINCE TIME CAPSULES RESEMBLE BURIED TREASURE, MAYBE JOINING THE GLOBAL TREASURE HUNT (#14) IS YOUR NEXT CHALLENGE!

27

SLEEP LIKE A CHAMPION

Have you ever thought how strange it is that every single day, you can't even remember what happens for hours? Or that during that time your body is more or less paralyzed and you go through strange, virtual-reality adventures called dreams?

Yes, we're talking about sleep. And it's just about the strangest thing that ever happens to us. But because it's so common, we often don't think about it at all.

Maybe because we take sleep for granted, it's easy to forget how important it is. If you don't get decent sleep, it's almost impossible to be a happy person, to learn much, or to be a good friend. Without enough sleep, most people feel stressed out, have trouble concentrating, and are more likely to get sick or even feel depressed.

So it's worth paying attention to these normal-but-strange hours in our day. With a little bit of science, you can make sure you're sleeping well, which in turn makes just about every other part of your life better.

GETTING STARTED

1 **How much sleep?** The current best research says that middle schoolers need around 9.25 hours of sleep per night. That's an average—some people need a little more or a little less. If you have to get up early for school, then most of the work to improve sleep is about how to go to sleep earlier. And yes, it's true: most schools start *way* too early.

2 **What you can do.** Watching a screen, any kind of screen, can keep your body too awake with its brightness. Try to stop screens at least a half-hour before you want to fall asleep. Same with eating—if you eat right before bed, your digestion process can make it harder to sleep well. Try to eat dinner at around the same time every day, ideally at least 2 hours before you sleep. Last but not least, try to make time to move your body. If you're stuck in a chair most of the day, chances are your body needs to move more in order to slee well.

3 **Challenge mode.** Could you get 9.25 hours of sleep per night, every night, for a solid week? That way you can put the science to the test and see if it makes a difference in how you feel. The challenge is getting your body ready to go to sleep earlier, since puberty changes your brain to make you more alert later at night.

4 **Explorer mode.** Sleep isn't just for resting. It's also home to one of your brain's great mysteries: *dreams*. Want to explore them? If you keep a notebook next to your bed, and set a goal to write about a dream as soon as you wake up, you'll likely improve your dream recall. Some dreams are just plain strange, but others might give you clues about what's on your mind, and definitely make for an interesting conversation with friends.

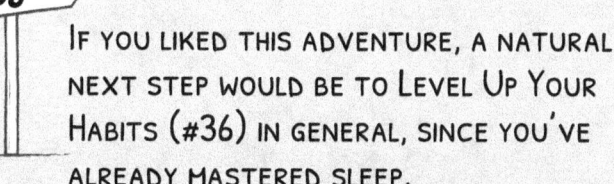

36 If you liked this adventure, a natural next step would be to Level Up Your Habits (#36) in general, since you've already mastered sleep.

35 Take it even further by Training Your Brain (#35). And just for fun, what if you discovered what it was like to

38 Sleep under the Stars (#38)?

28

BUILD SOMETHING FROM SCRATCH

Here's a strange fact: 99% of us live in spaces that someone else built, and we have no idea how they did it. Most of us don't know how to build a house, a car, or most anything.

What if you built something yourself—from the beginning?

Obviously we're not talking about building a house or a car from scratch. You can start with something much easier. What if you built a birdhouse or a model car, or even a simple shelter?

It's amazing how good it feels to learn how to put some tools to use. Then you can enjoy that weirdly wonderful sight: an idea in your head now exists as an actual real thing in the world.

GETTING STARTED

1 **What's worth building?** Is there something you've been wanting to build? Or a problem you could solve by building or fixing something yourself? It might help to brainstorm first and then sketch a few ideas. Some people enjoy doing this step with a friend or an adult with building skills.

2 **Details, details.** Now that you have some ideas, you can think about which ones are possible with the tools and skills you have and narrow your brainstorm list down to one good idea. You could call it Version 1. Which tools, materials, and skills are needed? It's OK if you don't have all the skills now—you can find people who have them, or find tutorials at the library or online.

3 **Gathering tools and helpers.** Once you have that list of tools, materials, and skills, you can start gathering them, along with your helpers—people who might give you a boost by sharing a skill, letting you borrow their gear, or giving you some feedback on your design idea.

4 **Test build.** Time to start building! If possible, before making the real thing, try making a *test build*. Think of it like a rough draft for your project, where you can try out your ideas and make mistakes without worrying about the final product. Once you're done, you'll clearly see what's working and what can be improved.

5 **The real deal.** Now that you have some experience from your test build, it's time to build the real thing. Just remember to be kind and patient with yourself—if it doesn't look perfect, this is just Version 1. Every future version (Version 2, 3, or more!) will be even better as your skills improve.

25

IF YOU LIKED THIS ADVENTURE, YOU MIGHT LOVE BUILDING THINGS IN GENERAL, IN WHICH CASE YOU COULD DESIGN THE ULTIMATE TEST (#25).

40

LEVEL UP EVEN MORE BY BECOMING AN APPRENTICE (#40) TO SOMEONE WITH EPIC BUILDING SKILLS.

29

DISCOVER WISDOM FROM AN ELDER

You're probably a *lot* smarter than you were five years ago. And think about how much smarter you'll be when you're 20. And then even smarter when you're 30.

So fast forward to 80, and imagine how much someone knows. About life, about what actually matters, about handling hard things. A lifetime's worth of wisdom.

If you want to, you could pick up some of this wisdom for yourself. You could interview someone over 80 about their life, their opinions, their ups and downs, and learn a ton as a result. And the surprising thing is that it's not asking a lot of them — chances are it would be a pleasure for them to share some stories.

Here's one other reason. Life gets so intense when everyone around you has the same worries. Like if you're 14 and everyone you spend time with is also 14, then you might think that the worries of a 14-year-old are the most important things in the world. When you zoom out of your perspective, you see things more clearly. That's what this challenge can do.

GETTING STARTED

1 **Who do you know?** Chances are, you don't have to look far to find someone this age. Maybe they're in your family, or your neighborhood, or a friend's family. Is there someone this old who seems interesting to you? If you're not sure, you could mention that you're doing this challenge to a few adults and see who they might suggest.

2 **What will you ask?** Before you interview them, it helps to create a list of questions. You could include some simple ones, like where they were born, but this is your chance to ask what you're *really* curious about. Maybe it's what they were worried about when they were your age, or what they wanted to be when they grew up? You could ask about what they would tell their younger self if they could go back in time, or when were they most afraid and how they handled it. Don't forget to ask them about the most exciting experience of their lives so far or the coolest thing they ever did.

3 **It's all about stories.** With thoughtful questions, you're going to hear some really good stories. People *love* sharing stories. Anyone over 80 has some amazing ones. You might even want to consider recording this and acting as a reporter or story-gatherer. You could document their stories on audio, video, or in writing.

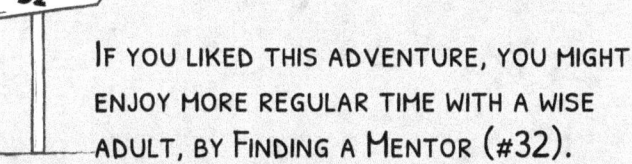

32

IF YOU LIKED THIS ADVENTURE, YOU MIGHT ENJOY MORE REGULAR TIME WITH A WISE ADULT, BY FINDING A MENTOR (#32).

19

OR REVERSE COURSE AND GO BACK INTO YOUR FAMILY'S HISTORY, BY CONNECTING WITH AN ANCESTOR (#19).

22

THE CRAZIEST IDEA IS REALIZING THAT *YOU* MIGHT BE THAT ELDER TO SOMEONE ELSE IF YOU SHARE WHAT YOU KNOW (#22).

30
PUBLISH YOUR WORK

What if you could be a published author before high school? Have a song on Spotify? Record a podcast that people listen to all over the world?

Believe it or not, all of these things are possible. If you're willing to work on it (and can get a bit of help along the way), you can see your work out there in the world, hear from readers or listeners about how it affected them, and make a difference to people.

There's another reason this can be awesome: it breaks a rule that needed to go. The rule that only adults can publish things, even when those things are for kids. This just isn't true—you can publish your own work, and what you create might be exactly what someone else is looking for.

GETTING STARTED

1 **How do you like to be creative?** Are you into writing stories, or making podcasts, or recording songs, or creating illustrations, or something else?

2 **What's your platform?** Your answer to the first question will guide you toward the right platform to publish your work. Writing a book? Anyone can create and publish a professional-quality book via Amazon (look for Kindle Direct Publishing). Making music? Anyone can post to Spotify or Bandcamp. Recording a podcast? Anyone can post to Apple Podcasts, Podbean, Buzzsprout, and many other options. Fan fiction? Try Wattpad. Making videos? There's YouTube. The list goes on!

3 **Create playfully.** Artists know that perfection is never possible—it's not even a good goal. If you make something that *you* would love to find, then someone receiving it will love it too. To get there, you may want to look for the feeling of *hard fun*. Creating should be fun, but also hard at times. The trick is to keep tinkering, asking for feedback, refining it, and then sharing it with the world *before it's perfect*.

4 **Tell people about it!** It would be sad if you did all the work of publishing something but then no one saw it! That's why it's essential to tell friends, family, teachers and others about where to find your published work. It can feel awkward, but these are the people who are cheering for you already — they're going to love it.

5 **Bonus challenge.** If you want your work to be truly high-quality, the key is to get the right feedback. Even the best writers in the world have editors. Even the greatest singers record their songs many times over to get it just right. If you can find a few people who are really good at the type of creative project you're making, they might be willing to give you a few specific suggestions to make your work better.

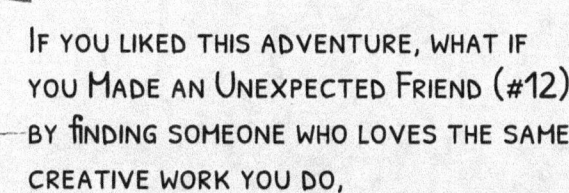

12

IF YOU LIKED THIS ADVENTURE, WHAT IF YOU MADE AN UNEXPECTED FRIEND (#12) BY fINDING SOMEONE WHO LOVES THE SAME CREATIVE WORK YOU DO,

7

OR BROADENED YOUR HORIZONS BY READING THE WORLD (#7)?

49

MAYBE IT'S THE INDEPENDENCE OF THIS CHALLENGE THAT fIRES YOU UP—YOU COULD LEAN INTO THAT BY BEING YOUR OWN BOSS (#49).

31
FORGIVE SOMEONE

Got any grudges? Someone you don't even want to think about? Or that feeling that you just can't trust someone ever again? If you do, welcome to the club. It's the most understandable thing in the world to have a grudge when you've been hurt.

Except there's one little problem: sometimes the grudges end up hurting *you* more. You might spend a lot of energy on them, continually feeling angry and resentful. Holding a grudge is like carrying a brick in your backpack every day. It's exhausting.

If you're ready to drop one of those bricks, practicing forgiveness is a good option. Letting go of a grudge doesn't mean saying it was okay for someone to hurt you. It just means accepting that they messed up. Chances are they're not as bad as they seem right now. They're probably a human who did something dumb. Even if they never become a friend, imagine how good it would feel to take that brick out of your backpack, worry less about them, and walk lighter.

GETTING STARTED

1 **Be honest.** Have you ever accidentally hurt someone? If not, then you need to win the next Nobel Peace Prize. We all make mistakes—it's part of being human. Take someone who constantly says hurtful things. You can bet they're repeating things that were said to them. Chances are they say even worse things to themselves in their own head. That doesn't make it OK, but it does make them human, and maybe a little more relatable.

2 **Say hi to your feelings.** It's okay to feel anger, sadness, shame, or any combination of emotions about what happened.

3 **Can you imagine forgiveness?** If you made a mistake like theirs, how would you want others to treat you? Forgiveness doesn't happen instantly, but you can start by imagining it. Maybe you could tell yourself *I can imagine forgiving them one day* or *I don't think they intended to hurt me at first.* You don't have to forgive anyone on their timeline, either—when you're ready, it begins with just imagining that you could let go of your grudge.

4 **One small step?** You don't *have* to tell them you forgive them. The most important work happens in your own heart. Still, small steps can help: writing a letter (even if you don't send it), talking to someone about it, or just journaling about how you feel. Starting to forgive makes your life less full of anger. And as crazy as it sounds, someone who seems like an enemy now might even become a friend in the future.

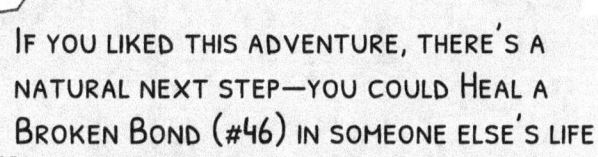

46 IF YOU LIKED THIS ADVENTURE, THERE'S A NATURAL NEXT STEP—YOU COULD HEAL A BROKEN BOND (#46) IN SOMEONE ELSE'S LIFE

45 OR EVEN STAND UP FOR SOMEONE (#45) BEFORE DAMAGE IS DONE.

3 AND TO REALLY MAKE THIS EXPERIENCE STICK, NOTHING BEATS WRITING ABOUT IT BY BEGINNING A JOURNAL (#3).

32

FIND A MENTOR

What if you knew a wizard who no one else could even see, and you could ask them for help anytime you want? That would be pretty awesome.

Although wizards aren't *exactly* real, there is a close human version. Someone who is wise, helpful, gives good advice, has your back no matter what, and doesn't have all the complications of being, say, your parent. That person is a *mentor*.

A mentor can be anyone willing to support you and challenge you to be your best self. They give you hints about how to get where you want to go. They might help you in pretty direct ways too, like finding an after-school job or handling a friendship problem. The best mentors listen to you, share their own ups and downs, and can make any problem or dream you have seem more manageable or achievable.

It can take a few tries to find the right mentor. The first person you ask might not be the right fit. But if you keep at it, you *will* find your mentor. You'll know it when you feel both excited and slightly nervous to be around them, or when you're amazed that they're willing to give you their time. They might not be able to do magic, but a good mentor is as close to a wizard as you can find.

GETTING STARTED

1 **Look around you.** Is there someone already in your life—like an aunt, uncle, coach, or past teacher—who could be the right mentor, but just needs to be asked? If you feel connected to an adult, start there. You can begin by asking if they would be up for talking once in a while about life, or by asking them one of the questions on your mind.

2 **Find a program.** If you haven't found someone already in your life, you could look for mentoring programs. There are organizations like Big Brothers Big Sisters, the Boys & Girls Clubs, local youth centers, or civic associations like Rotary or Lions Clubs. You could also ask a counselor, teacher, or coach if they know of a good program.

3 **Ask for recommendations.** If those methods haven't worked, you could ask trusted adults—like parents, teachers, family friends, coaches, or relatives—to help you find a mentor. While you're waiting, keep your eyes open. As you talk to the adults around you each day, you can keep asking yourself, does one seem especially cool or inspiring? If you keep looking and asking others for help with this, you will find someone. And it's worth it – that person might become one of your most trusted guides in life.

41

IF YOU LIKED THIS ADVENTURE, YOU COULD BE EVEN BOLDER BY ASKING FOR HONEST FEEDBACK (#41).

29

IF YOU'D LIKE SOME MORE PRO TIPS FROM A WISE ADULT, WHY NOT DISCOVER WISDOM FROM AN ELDER (#29)?

36

AND TO PUT THAT WISDOM INTO ACTION, CONSIDER THE CHALLENGE OF LEVELING UP YOUR HABITS (#36).

33

PLOT A TRAVEL ADVENTURE

Some adventures just happen to you. Others you get to create. And what might be surprising is that for some adventures, the planning is one of the best parts.

Let's say you want to go on a road trip with your family. Maybe that can't happen right away. But planning it can be almost as much fun as the real thing. You might research the coolest sights to see and build a map of your ideal route. Each time you work on planning it, part of you is already going on an adventure.

Maybe your adventure is closer to home. After all, most of us live near cool places we haven't explored yet — parks, towns, museums, hiking trails, or other hidden gems. You could figure out how to take public transportation there with friends, working out costs, routes, and where to stop for food. Then you get to enjoy it twice — once in your imagination and then again in real life!

GETTING STARTED

1 **Blank page or a menu?** Some people like to start with a blank page, imagining an ideal trip and then figuring out how to make it happen. Others like to see their options, like looking at a menu at a restaurant, and get inspired by what's available. Both are great. What works for you? If you want to see a list, you could ask friends and family members for destination ideas, borrow travel books from a library, or do some online research to discover your options.

2 **Who is with you?** If you're planning a family trip, how can you include something for each person to enjoy? If it's with friends, what will they love the most? Giving people choices can help them feel included and as excited as you are about the adventure.

3 **Make a plan.** Travel planning involves a ton of details—which can even be part of the fun. Nailing down those details helps you imagine each step of the journey. You may want to make a budget, look up travel options like bus or train schedules, consider driving distances, and make backup plans in case of bad weather. A fun challenge for someone who loves travel planning is to figure out how much you can do for free. You may be amazed at how much is possible!

4 **Hit the road!** Sometimes the best plans are just the starting point, and once you're on the adventure, things change! If that happens, that's ok. It's a good idea not to be too set on every detail of your plan, because you may discover unexpected awesome things along the way. Each trip is like an experiment, showing you what you love and where to find it.

37

IF YOU LIKED THIS ADVENTURE, YOU MIGHT BE READY FOR EVEN MORE TRAVEL — WHAT IF YOU WALK INTO THE UNKNOWN (#37)

38

OR VENTURE INTO THE WILDERNESS BY SLEEPING UNDER THE STARS (#38)?

49

IF IT'S THE INDEPENDENCE THAT SPEAKS TO YOU, IT COULD BE TIME TO TRY BEING YOUR OWN BOSS (#49).

34

TALK ON THE BRIGHT SIDE

Are you feeling like life is *too* easy? Then this is the challenge for you, because it is, well, insanely hard. Like borderline impossible. Honestly, you might want to skip this chapter entirely. (Still here? Okay, you've been warned.)

Here's why this one is so hard—because life is full of so many annoying things! Like super-*frustrating*. Borderline *infuriating*. So it's no surprise that we get into the habit of talking—and thinking—negatively. The problem? We get stuck there. It becomes automatic. We complain and criticize. We talk to ourselves in ways that would count as *bullying* if someone else said it out loud.

Here's an example. Let's say your internet goes down—everyone would agree that it's annoying, right? So sure, focus on it. But if you were really balanced in your thinking, you would be *thankful* for every single day the internet worked before now. Were you? Probably not. That's because we tend to notice the occasional negative more than the almost-always positive. This challenge flips the script.

Here's your mission: For one full day, try to avoid using negative language *of any kind*. That means no complaining, no criticizing, no putting yourself or others down. Instead, practice finding something positive to say about every situation—even the tough ones. It might sound simple, but it's an intense workout for your brain.

GETTING STARTED

1 **Choose the day.** It helps to pick this ahead of time so you can get yourself ready for the challenge.

2 **Have an accountability buddy.** Who is someone you trust— someone who can keep it real with you? This could be someone your age or an adult. You can ask them to be your accountability buddy for this challenge, meaning that their job is to remind you and help you stick with this for a full day, and talk with you about how it went afterward.

3 **Stick with it.** The goal of this challenge is not perfection. Almost no one could truly avoid all negative language for a full day on their first try. The goal is just to get as close as you can. As an old Japanese saying goes, *Fall down 7 times, get up 8*. It doesn't matter how many times you slip up and accidentally use negative language. What matters is that each time you notice it, you refocus. You're building a special kind of muscle—one that helps your mind see the good in the world.

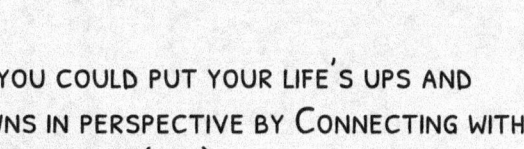

35

IF YOU LIKED THIS ADVENTURE, YOU'RE ALREADY WELL ON YOUR WAY TO TRAINING YOUR BRAIN (#35).

41

AN UNEXPECTED TWIST MIGHT BE TO ASK FOR HONEST FEEDBACK (#41).

19

OR YOU COULD PUT YOUR LIFE'S UPS AND DOWNS IN PERSPECTIVE BY CONNECTING WITH AN ANCESTOR (#19).

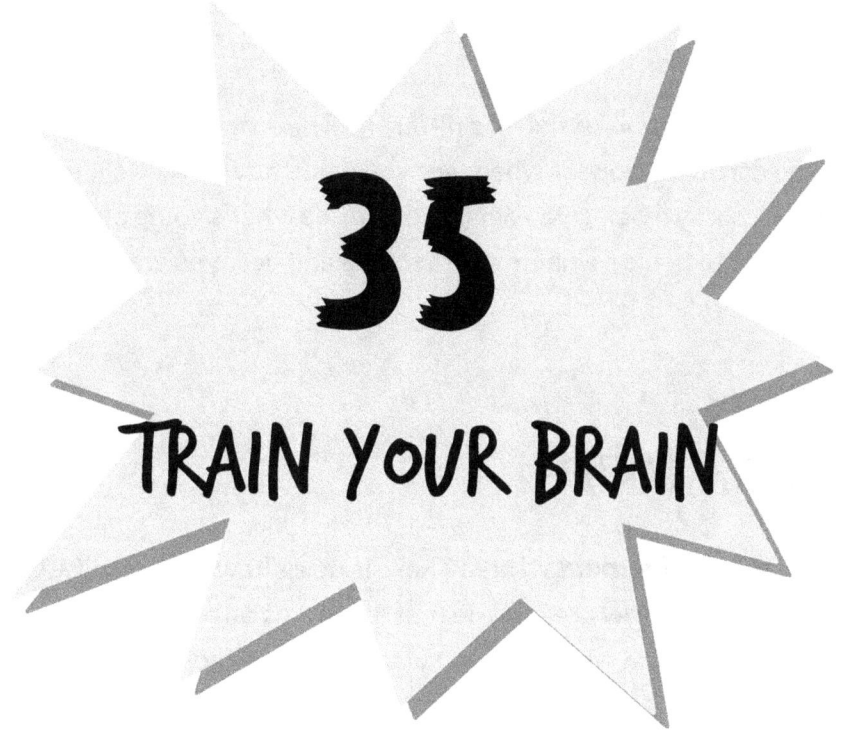

35
TRAIN YOUR BRAIN

Meditation might be one of the weirdest things you could ever do.

People tend to think that it means sitting down silently and never moving, and more or less trying *not* to think. No one would blame you for imagining that sounds both insanely boring and impossibly hard at the same time.

But what if you thought of meditation as a special kind of training—in *how to be you*. Not the version of you that reacts without thinking, but the *real* you. A lot of what we do every day is driven by emotions or outside pressure. Anger makes us snap, anxiety keeps us quiet, and boredom pushes us to scroll or snack. When you're just controlled by your reactions, then you (I hate to say it) are a bit like a *zombie*. You go on wanting, avoiding, and reacting without necessarily getting to *be you*.

Meditation gives you something different. Think of it like a doorway that you can make appear whenever you want, and if you walk through it, you get back to being you again. You notice what's going on inside, and you get to decide what matters to you and how you want to show up in the world.

GETTING STARTED

1 **Letting go of expectations.** There is no right way to meditate. The options below are just the first few items on a long menu. You can try them whenever you want to feel calmer or more like yourself.

2 **The classic.** This works for some people and not others. It involves sitting down on the floor (maybe on a cushion). Let your back be straight and tall, but keep your shoulders relaxed. Close your eyes or focus them gently on something in front of you. Then, take slow, deep breaths in through your nose and exhale out through your mouth. Thoughts are going to pop into your head. When they do, you can just let them float by, without getting wrapped up in them, like watching clouds drifting in the sky. If you can do this for even 1-2 minutes, you're doing great.

3 **The tasty.** This is a totally different way to meditate. It's simple: find one piece of food you really like, ideally something fresh, like a ripe strawberry. Sit down, and put the strawberry in front of you. Close your eyes. Then, eat the strawberry as slowly as you possibly can. Experience every little bit of it. That's it!

4 **Meditation to go.** This is also called walking meditation. Find a quiet place where no one can make you self-conscious by watching you. Stand up tall, with shoulders relaxed. Then *walk*. Only this time (maybe for the first time ever) you aren't walking to get anywhere. You're just walking to enjoy walking. It sounds strange, but it can be oddly relaxing. As you walk, try to breathe slowly and deeply. When thoughts come up, notice them and let them go, like leaves floating down a stream.

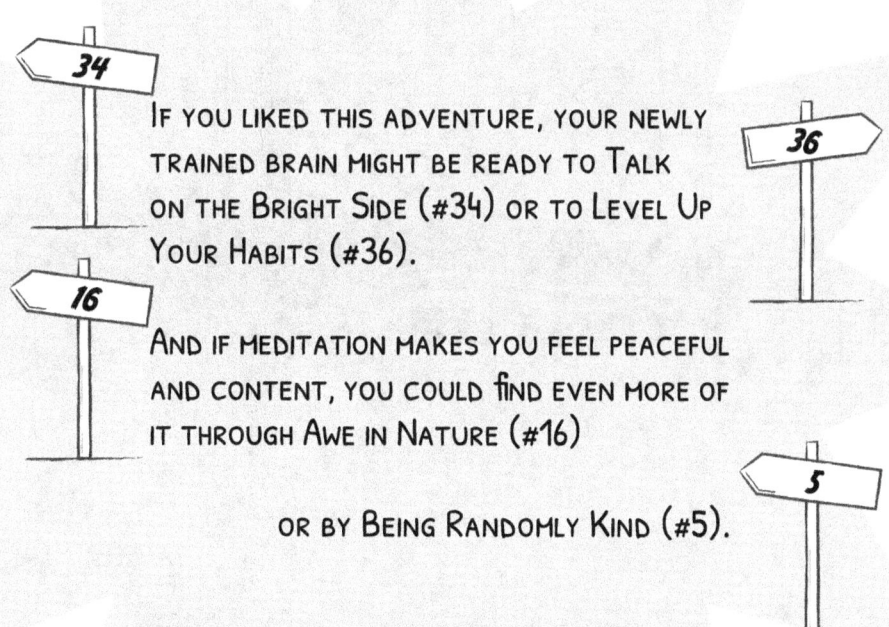

34

IF YOU LIKED THIS ADVENTURE, YOUR NEWLY TRAINED BRAIN MIGHT BE READY TO TALK ON THE BRIGHT SIDE (#34) OR TO LEVEL UP YOUR HABITS (#36).

36

16

AND IF MEDITATION MAKES YOU FEEL PEACEFUL AND CONTENT, YOU COULD FIND EVEN MORE OF IT THROUGH AWE IN NATURE (#16)

OR BY BEING RANDOMLY KIND (#5).

5

36

LEVEL UP YOUR HABITS

Habits are almost *too* powerful. Bad ones can hold you back. Even normal ones can control you. But the *good* ones—the ones you build on purpose— can be almost superpowers.

We all have habits that help us and ones that don't. The tricky part isn't spotting them—it's changing them. Maybe you want to start something new, or maybe you want to stop a habit that isn't helping anymore. Both are totally possible. The awesome part is that once you realize you can change your habits, you'll know how to transform almost any part of your life.

So if you want to be the master of your habits instead of letting them master you, it's time to practice. There are a few tricks to make changes stick, and once you learn them, you're in the driver's seat.

GETTING STARTED

1 Pick your habit. What's one habit you'd like to build—or break? If you're not sure, look for that guilty feeling when you do something you know isn't great for you. Or, think of something you *wish* you did more often. You can also ask a friend or trusted adult to suggest one habit you could do more of, and one habit you might want to do less of.

2 What's your goal? It helps to make your goal as specific as possible, so you know if you're succeeding. You may want to include how you'll track your progress, and a date for when you hope to have met the goal. For example: *I want to be able to do 25 push-ups by the time the next school year starts. I'll write down on my calendar how many I did each day.*

3 How will you remind yourself? We all need help to stay focused on a goal, especially a new one. It can help to create specific reminders for yourself that you'll see every day, like a note on your door. It also helps to work on your habit at the same time and place each day. And if you're trying to break a bad habit, a helpful trick is to replace it with a better one at the same time of day—like drinking ice water with lemon instead of a sugary soda every afternoon after school.

4 **Finding a habit buddy.** Changes are more doable—and more fun—when shared with a supportive friend. When you don't feel like working on it, sometimes knowing that your friend will check in might give you that extra boost you need.

5 **How will you celebrate?** It can take a lot of time and effort to change a habit, so it's worth rewarding yourself when you do. It can help to plan a special treat in advance, maybe with your habit buddy, so you have something to look forward to when you reach your goal.

35

IF YOU LIKED THIS ADVENTURE, YOU MIGHT BE READY FOR ONE OF THE ULTIMATE HABITS: TRAINING YOUR BRAIN (#35).

27

OR YOU COULD BUILD THAT CORE HABIT THAT MAKES EVERYTHING ELSE BETTER—LEARNING TO SLEEP LIKE A CHAMPION (#27).

37

WALK INTO THE UNKNOWN

So you think you know the place you live?

OK, so you probably know your block, maybe some parks near you, even the area around your school or friends' homes. But actually, if you really think about it, that's a pretty tiny area. Most of us just stay in the same few places.

You might be surprised at how much more there is right around you. People, stores, views, interesting streets, beautiful parks—it's pretty much guaranteed that there is so much around you that you've never seen.

The catch is that the *way* we move around can make it hard to notice. If you're zooming by in a car or bus, or on a bike or train, you're going to miss most of it.

If you really want to see the world, try *walking*. That's the pace that lets you notice *everything*. The people, the shops, the homes, the streets, the plants, and even the conversations around you. Going for a long walk will probably amaze you with how much is new. You'll cross neighborhoods, maybe even walk straight out of your town. You'll become a better navigator and your world will expand. And the best discoveries are often just around the corner you've never turned.

GETTING STARTED

1 **A good map.** Begin by getting your hands on a map. This could be a physical map or a digital one on a phone. You could pick interesting landmarks to see or new neighborhoods to explore. It helps to plan your route in advance. You could also challenge yourself with a specific distance, like aiming to walk for 1 or 2 miles — or for ultimate challenge level, go for 5!

2 **The right gear.** Your future self will probably thank you for bringing snacks, water, maybe a camera or journal to document cool finds, and some spending money for unexpected treasures along your journey.

3 **A walking buddy?** Exploring with a friend or family member can make the adventure even more fun—and it's awesome to share discoveries as you go.

4 **Street smarts.** A little preparation goes a long way. Make sure to get your parents' ok for this adventure, have a phone or a plan for reaching out to someone (it's wise to have at least one phone number memorized so you can reach an adult at any time), and locate some safe spots like libraries or cafés along your route. Your parents can help you think through what makes sense for your community.

IF YOU LIKED THIS ADVENTURE, YOU MIGHT ENJOY EVEN BIGGER UNKNOWNS BY MAKING AN UNEXPECTED FRIEND (#12).

OR IF IT'S DISCOVERY THAT LIGHTS YOU UP, YOU MIGHT BE READY TO TRY A NEW HOLIDAY (#15)

OR EXPLORE AN UNFAMILIAR RELIGION (#24).

38

SLEEP UNDER THE STARS

If you've never slept under the stars, out in the wilderness far from towns and busy streets, you may be missing one of the most magical experiences available on this planet.

Why might this be awesome? There's a strange but maybe obvious reason. *Humans don't come from towns and cities!* Our species evolved in the wilderness. All of our senses work best there. And once we're used to it, we tend to feel less anxious and more alive when we're in nature.

But since most of us didn't grow up in the wilderness, we actually became afraid of our own original home! What a plot twist.

But this creates an opportunity for you. If you can find a way to get comfortable in nature, it's like activating a set of secret superpowers. You might start to feel more comfortable in general, more skillful and resourceful, and more aware of how beautiful our planet is.

Going for a hike or taking in a beautiful view are great steps. But to *really* feel the magic of nature, try spending a night in the wilderness. Maybe you'll see the stars more clearly than you ever have. Maybe you'll face some fears and come out stronger. It's quite possible you'll have a once-in-a-lifetime adventure.

GETTING STARTED

1 **Adventure buddies.** If you don't yet have much outdoor experience, chances are good that someone around you does. Maybe a relative, family member, or someone in a friend's family is into hiking and camping. Maybe there's an outdoor program near you, and a teacher could point you in the right direction. Once you find someone who really loves camping and is willing to introduce you to it, you're most of the way there.

2 **Nature skills.** This is one of the most fun parts, because you can watch your skills grow fast. As you get ready for your first (or next) camping adventure, you can practice key skills like how to set up a tent, store and prepare food (camp food always tastes extra good), safely build a campfire, navigate outdoors, or identify plants and animals.

3 **Adventure time.** With some new skills and an experienced friend or group up for an adventure, you're ready for action. There's so much to do and experience on a camping trip. You can explore on foot, discover trails and streams, climb trees, start a campfire if it's allowed, and make yourself a simple meal. You could identify which birds are singing near you, even collect plants for tea, and curl up in your sleeping bag in the evening to read a good book or tell stories. And don't forget to check out the stars after dark — it's amazing how many you can see on a clear night in the wilderness!

16

IF YOU LIKED THIS ADVENTURE, IT MAY LEAD YOU RIGHT TO FINDING AWE IN NATURE (#16)—

33

WHICH YOU CAN find EVEN MORE OF WHEN YOU PLOT A TRAVEL ADVENTURE (#33).

48

ALL THESE OUTDOOR ADVENTURES MIGHT GIVE YOU A DESIRE TO PROTECT ANIMALS — IN WHICH CASE YOU MIGHT SURPRISE YOURSELF BY WANTING TO RESCUE AN ANIMAL (#48).

39

STICK OUT IN A GROUP

Ever had that nightmare where everyone is staring at you and you're not sure why? It's a common one. Probably because for most humans, sticking out can feel terrifying. We all want to belong.

But there's a problem here — being too scared to stick out can end up hurting you. In order to be accepted, you might start hiding parts of yourself. Like dropping a hobby you really love, just in case your friends think it's uncool. Or being unkind to someone because your friends don't like them. It can get pretty rough.

So how do you break free of this? Here's the challenge: instead of always hanging out with people you know well, what if you chose to spend time in a group where you stand out?

It might feel uncomfortable at first. Actually, it *will* feel uncomfortable. But that's why you get stronger as a result. It's like going to the gym. That muscle you're building is your confidence to *be you* in any group. You'll also get better at making friends, which has to be one of the most useful skills any human could have. You'll even learn how to be awkward for a minute and not let it stop you.

GETTING STARTED

1 **Find a group.** This could be a club where everyone has different interests from you, or maybe where people are older than you. Or a group playing a sport or game you don't yet know how to play. The key is finding people who are welcoming and interested in others joining their group.

2 **Need some ideas?** Think about clubs at school or in your town that might be looking for new members. Maybe you've never tried debate before, or played Dungeons & Dragons, or acted on stage. But if the people in the club are friendly, this could be your moment.

3 **Look for a connection.** Maybe you have a friend in one of these clubs or activities, but don't know most of the other people there. That counts—as long as you don't only talk to your friend! Or maybe a friend could invite you to a place where they have special access, like a sports league or their church's community potluck.

4 **Use your new powers.** Once you've felt what it's like to be the different one, you can become a champion for others. Next time you see someone feeling awkward—maybe it's the kid in dance class who looks like they want to disappear, or the student who just moved from a different country—*you* could be the one who makes them feel welcome. That's the superpower you've been training for.

45

IF YOU LIKED THIS ADVENTURE, YOU HAVE SOME BOLDNESS TO YOU, SO YOU'RE PROBABLY READY TO STAND UP FOR SOMEONE (#45).

43

YOU MIGHT EVEN BE ABLE TO PROPOSE A BETTER RULE (#43).

42

AND LEARNING TO HANDLE AWKWARD MOMENTS MAKES YOU READY TO MASTER FINDING SHELTER IN EMOTIONAL STORMS (#42).

40
BECOME AN APPRENTICE

Did you know that before there were schools, before Math and English classes even existed, there was another way that people got an education? It's called an *apprenticeship*. It means learning directly from someone who's already mastered a skill, by doing it alongside them.

If you think about it, everywhere around you there are people who have amazing skills. Someone who can design software from scratch. Someone who can take a few tubes of paint and create art. Or someone who can turn a broken-down heap of a car into a smoothly-running vehicle.

Chances are you have neighbors or family members with incredible skills like these. If you want to learn from them, sometimes all you have to do is ask.

GETTING STARTED

1 **Choose an interest.** You can learn just about anything with an apprenticeship. Do you have a passion, an idea of a job you'd like one day, or a skill you're curious about? It's fine if you don't know much about it yet, since this challenge is all about exploring.

2 **Who do you know?** Even if you don't know the right person yet, chances are *someone you know* does. You could start by making a list of people to ask, including extended family, your friends' families, neighbors, and people your parents know. If you let them know that you're looking for an apprenticeship in a specific skill or subject, they can help you. You could also write up a short description to share with your network, describing who you are and why you want to learn a specific skill. The secret is that people have a hard time saying no to a motivated young person who has a real passion.

3 **What's your request?** When you've found someone who might be interested in offering an apprenticeship, it helps to make a specific, polite request. For example, after explaining why you're interested in their job or hobby, you could ask if they would consider allowing you to visit on Wednesday afternoons after school for the next month, to observe them working, to help out, and to ask questions. The details will depend on the activity, your host's schedule, and your own. Offering to help with small tasks can show you're serious. It would be a nice touch to thank them for even considering the request. The more you show your interest and enthusiasm, the more likely you are to get a yes.

4 **What's your plan?** Once someone has agreed to offer you an apprenticeship (congratulations!), the next step is to make a really clear, specific plan. Ideally, that would include completing a project together to focus the experience, with a schedule of when you'll meet. Talk about what you want to learn and what they expect from you—this keeps everyone happy. Then it's time for action!

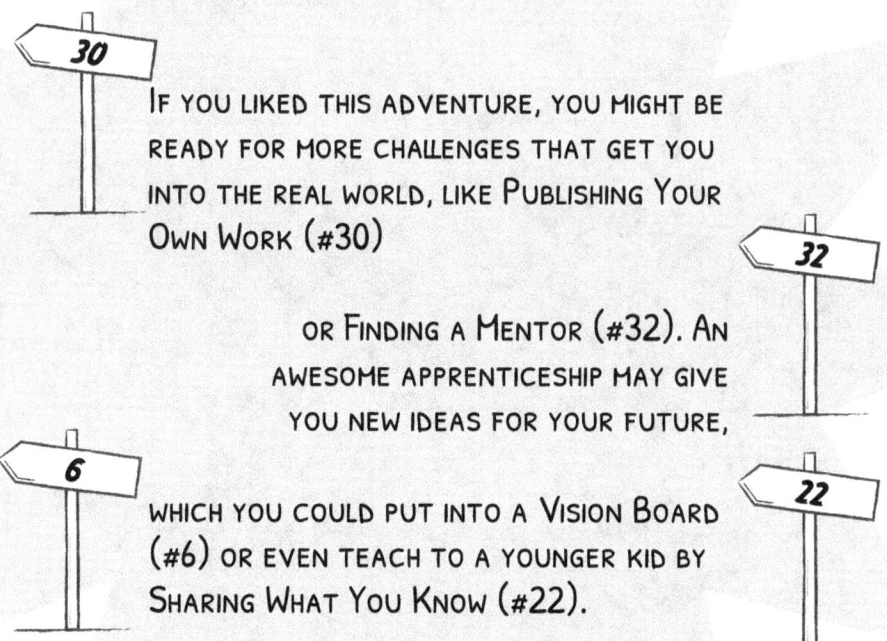

30

IF YOU LIKED THIS ADVENTURE, YOU MIGHT BE READY FOR MORE CHALLENGES THAT GET YOU INTO THE REAL WORLD, LIKE PUBLISHING YOUR OWN WORK (#30)

32

OR FINDING A MENTOR (#32). AN AWESOME APPRENTICESHIP MAY GIVE YOU NEW IDEAS FOR YOUR FUTURE,

6

22

WHICH YOU COULD PUT INTO A VISION BOARD (#6) OR EVEN TEACH TO A YOUNGER KID BY SHARING WHAT YOU KNOW (#22).

41

ASK FOR HONEST FEEDBACK

If someone walked up and said *Hey, I've got some feedback for you*, how would you feel? If your answer was somewhere between *nervous* and *please no*, then this might be the challenge for you.

It's strange, but most of us are scared of feedback. We assume it will be negative, or that giving feedback is just a way for someone to say what they don't like about us.

Here's a different way to think about it. There are things about you that are obvious to others but *not to you*. For example, you might have a hard time naming all your strengths, but your friends or family could list them in seconds. Or think about that essay you wrote and can't stand to look at again before you turn it in—someone might see an easy improvement in 2 minutes.

But the problem is... *we don't ask*. It's like someone standing next to you is holding a treasure map, but we're too afraid to ask them to see it. So that's what this challenge is all about: asking.

GETTING STARTED

1 **General or specific feedback?** You could ask for feedback on a specific topic, like how to improve your basketball game or your writing. Or, you could ask for general feedback, with a question like *Could you help me identify two strengths of mine, and also one area that I could get better at? Or: What do you think I should do more of and what should I do less of to be at my best?* It might feel awkward to ask, but it will be worth it if you get some helpful ideas and prove to yourself that you aren't scared of feedback.

2 **Who will you ask?** Who is someone you trust, someone honest *and* kind, who won't turn feedback into criticism or pressure? For example, feedback from a parent can be awesome because they know you so well, but if you think you might get annoyed with what they say, then it may be better to ask someone else. Think of teachers, coaches, mentors, cousins, or good friends.

3 **Get ready.** Feedback is like getting a gift at a birthday party. Some are exactly what you wanted. Some you might never use. And some are weird surprises that turn out to be your favorite. The point is, you don't know what you'll get—but it's all information. Try to keep an open mind and remember that everyone sees you differently. You are still in control. You can ignore the feedback that isn't helpful.

4 **Ask and reflect.** It helps to ask at least two people, because it might be interesting if they say the same thing or see you in a different way. Then you can take some time to think about what you heard. Does it sound right to you? Does it help you understand yourself better? Some people like to reflect in a journal, or you may want to talk it through with a friend or adult. Either way, you just did something brave—and useful.

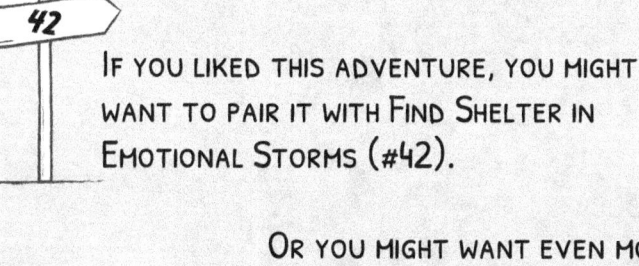

42 IF YOU LIKED THIS ADVENTURE, YOU MIGHT WANT TO PAIR IT WITH FIND SHELTER IN EMOTIONAL STORMS (#42).

32 OR YOU MIGHT WANT EVEN MORE HONEST FEEDBACK, WHICH COULD COME FROM FINDING A MENTOR (#32).

46 GETTING USED TO BRAVE CONVERSATIONS ALSO MAKES YOU AN IDEAL PERSON TO HEAL A BROKEN BOND (#46).

42

FIND SHELTER IN EMOTIONAL STORMS

Life gets intense sometimes. And we humans are emotional beings. Once in a while we all get stressed and overwhelmed.

Big emotions can feel like a storm rolling in. You can't always stop them. You might not even want to, because emotions often have something important to say. But there's a big difference between being outside during a storm and watching it from a safe, cozy shelter.

That's what this challenge is all about—finding the keys to your shelter so you can make it through an emotional storm. Once you're safely inside, you can think about what to make of the storm of emotions you feel, what the real problem is, and how to do something about it.

GETTING STARTED

1 **Breathing.** It sounds basic—and it is. That's the beauty of it! When you're stressed, your breathing gets faster and more shallow, which can make you feel *more* panicked. To slow it down, try this pattern: breathe in slowly for 5 seconds, hold the air inside for 5 seconds, then breathe out slowly for 5 seconds, and finally wait 5 seconds before breathing back in. If you do this for a few minutes, you may find it turns the volume down on worried thoughts.

2 **Movement.** It's easy to get wrapped up in our thoughts when we're upset, like imagining how mad someone is going to be at you. When that happens, it can really help to move your body in a way that feels good, like running, stretching, doing jumping jacks, even shaking your arms like a wet dog (seriously!).

3 **Nature.** When your thoughts are spinning, nature can bring you back to calm. Even a short walk in a place like a park, forest, or even a quiet street with trees can bring peaceful feelings. If you can find a spot like that, try taking ten minutes to refocus on the plants, colors, and other sights or sounds of nature around you.

4 **Journaling.** A journal can be like a secret friend—the truest and most loyal kind—always ready to listen without judging you. You can vent as much as you want or even write a letter to your future self.

5 **Empathy buddies.** Sometimes the best shelter is another person. If you have a friend, family member, or mentor who is a great listener—who can let you share your feelings and understand what you are saying—this may be your best bet.

6 **Distraction.** Sometimes our emotions are so big because the problems can't be solved right now. At those times it's OK to just distract ourselves until the storm dies down. That might mean reading, watching a funny show, doing something kind for someone else, or using your senses—smell something soothing, touch something soft, or listen to calming sounds or music.

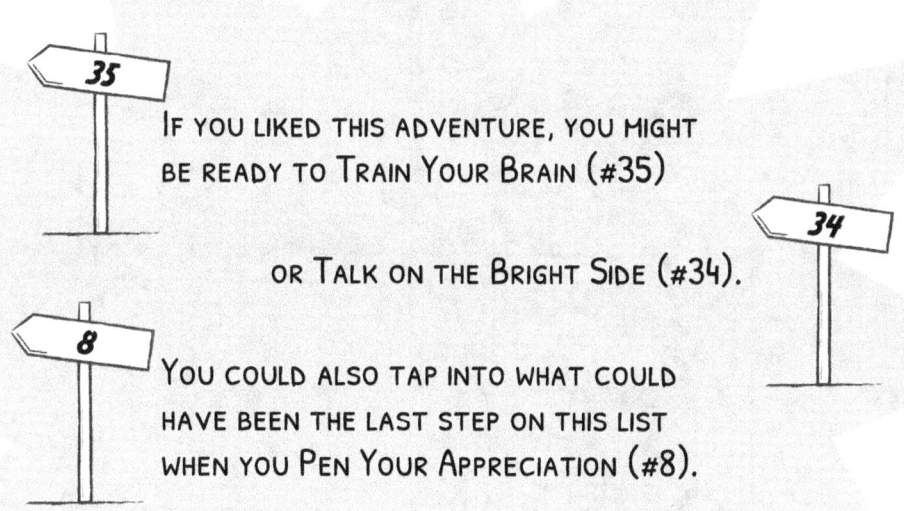

35

IF YOU LIKED THIS ADVENTURE, YOU MIGHT BE READY TO TRAIN YOUR BRAIN (#35)

34

OR TALK ON THE BRIGHT SIDE (#34).

8

YOU COULD ALSO TAP INTO WHAT COULD HAVE BEEN THE LAST STEP ON THIS LIST WHEN YOU PEN YOUR APPRECIATION (#8).

43

PROPOSE A BETTER RULE

Middle schoolers are underestimated by, well, just about everyone. One way you know that is by how adults tell middle schoolers what to do *all the time*. But what if you want to change a rule or suggest a better way to do something?

If you want to do that, you'll need to use your voice. The challenge is, sometimes when middle schoolers speak up, they get told they're complaining. So the trick is to turn that complaint into something more powerful and useful: into feedback.

What does it look like? Maybe there's a rule at school that you don't like. Your feedback could be a thoughtful letter to the principal, or a petition, which is a letter signed by many people all requesting the same change. Maybe there's a rule in your town or country that feels wrong, and your feedback could be anything from a letter-writing campaign to a protest.

One thing is for sure: the world needs feedback in order to get better. Why not have it come from you?

GETTING STARTED

1. **Who's in charge?** Once you have a bad rule or policy in mind, find out *who* can change it. That might mean the principal of your school, the mayor or council of your town, or the owner of a company.

2. **Giving your feedback.** To make sure your feedback is taken seriously, it helps to focus on your personal experience. You can use I statements (like *I would feel safer if our town built a bike path for kids like me to get to school*) to describe how a given situation has affected you. You should also avoid exaggerations. Words like *always*, *never*, and *everyone* can make you seem less serious.

3. **Make a proposal.** Once you've described the problem, you can then propose your solution—the more specific the better. It also helps to show that you're willing to listen to their point of view.

4. **What's the best format?** It could be a letter, a petition, a protest, a social media campaign, or simply a conversation. If you think you won't be taken seriously, it helps to have others on your side—either signing a letter together or joining forces to go to a meeting.

5 **Feedback on your feedback.** Before you present your ideas, it helps to practice what you're going to say or share a draft with a trusted friend to make sure it's clear and powerful.

6 **Be steadfast.** If the change is important, it's worth arguing for, even if it doesn't happen as fast as you want. When someone realizes you're going to keep asking for change and won't go away, they may eventually be willing to compromise.

47 IF YOU LIKED THIS ADVENTURE, YOU HAVE THE POWER TO MAKE CHANGE—ADD SOME BUSINESS SKILLS AND YOU'RE READY TO TURN CASH INTO CHANGE (#47).

11 YOUR ABILITY TO HELP OTHERS MIGHT ALSO MAKE YOU A NATURAL TO BECOME A CITIZEN SCIENTIST (#11).

25 DOING THINGS FOR OTHERS DOESN'T HAVE TO BE SERIOUS THOUGH — WHAT IF YOU DESIGNED THE ULTIMATE TEST (#25)?

44
START A MICROBUSINESS

You could open a classic lemonade stand. How fun would it be to see a jar fill up with money while customers enjoy your lemonade? Or you could become a dog walker, playing with furry friends *and* getting paid to do it.

These are just a few of the many businesses you could start. Others might be selling homemade desserts, taking care of people's yards, running a car-washing service, or even offering tutoring. The list is endless!

Whatever you decide to do, there is something powerful about making money yourself through your own hard work. You'll figure out how to create a product or offer a service, let people know about it, and manage the money that comes in. All of these are incredibly useful skills—and earning some cash is a nice bonus!

GETTING STARTED

1 **Matchmaking time.** Starting a business is a bit like matchmaking—you have skills, and someone out there needs help. Can you find a match between one of your skills and a need someone has? If it's hard to think of one, consider asking a few friends or adults. You might be surprised by what others see in you.

2 **Designing your product or service.** Once you have an idea for a match between someone's need and your skills, the next step is to plan out your product or service. That might mean thinking through what materials you need, or how to practice beforehand. For example, if you're starting a lemonade stand, you might make a to-do list: gather ingredients, find cups, locate a lemon squeezer, set up a table, and make an awesome sign.

3 **Finding your customers.** Telling people about your business can feel scary, but it's worth it. Which ways feel most comfortable to you? If you like to design or draw, you could create a poster or print flyers. You could send emails or ask your family to post online. The clearer you are about what kind of person needs your help, the easier it is to find them. You could explain what you're offering, your experience, the price, and where you can be found.

4 **Making customers happy.** Most great businesses succeed because happy customers tell other people. Say you walk your neighbor's dog and do a wonderful job—sooner or later they're going to tell a friend, and more customers will start appearing. At this stage, your job is just to make your customers happy and do great work. You'll earn a positive reputation, and eventually people will be lining up to hire you!

9

IF YOU LIKED THIS ADVENTURE, YOU COULD KEEP YOUR NEW CASH SAFE BY OPENING A BANK ACCOUNT (#9).

6

WHEN YOUR NEW BUSINESS IS GOING WELL, YOU MIGHT BE fiRED UP TO MAKE AN AWESOME VISION BOARD (#6)

47

OR EVEN TO PUT THOSE BUSINESS SKILLS TO GOOD USE BY TURNING CASH INTO CHANGE (#47).

45

STAND UP FOR SOMEONE

Have you ever thought that the world is really beautiful and also pretty messed up? Somehow both are true. And possibly the most messed-up times are when someone is being mistreated and everyone else just lets it happen.

There's even a name for this: the bystander effect. It's when people look the other way on purpose while something bad happens.

Could you act differently? Not just let it happen? It takes real bravery. But the bystander effect also has a surprising twist. As soon as one person starts to help and acts as an *ally*, the next person who was *almost* brave enough to help will jump in too. Things can get better—surprisingly fast.

It might feel scary, but think about how much the person you're speaking up for will appreciate it. And probably other people who were too scared to say something will admire what you did, and might be willing to speak up next time. Better world, here we come.

GETTING STARTED

1 **Who needs help?** Chances are you've already seen it: someone in your school or online who gets teased or bullied, maybe for being different. If you know someone like this, why not start there? You could let them know that it's not right how they're being treated and that you respect them. If possible, you could tell the people doing this to stop. Maybe they don't even realize the harm they're doing. If that's too risky, you could get help for them from a trusted adult.

2 **Stand up.** At any given moment, many people in the world are having a hard time. There are families escaping wars and leaving all their belongings behind, and people attacked just for being different. There are ways to help. If this inspires you, you could find organizations that are working to help them (through online research or by asking adults for suggestions). You could raise money or write letters to your elected leaders to tell them what's happening.

3 **Get ready.** If you don't see a need to stand up for someone now, it might help to get ready for when the time comes. If you plan ahead about what you would say, you're more likely to do it. For example, imagine a student is saying bad things about another student in a group text or online. You could say *Hey, let's keep it positive* or *Guys, this isn't cool.* You can even put it on your parents, saying *If my parents see this, they'll be super mad that we're talking to each other this way. Let's stop.*

46

IF YOU LIKED THIS ADVENTURE, YOU MIGHT LOVE HELPING OTHER PEOPLE, WHICH MEANS THAT HEALING A BROKEN BOND (#46) COULD BE PRETTY AWESOME.

43

YOU CAN EVEN STAND UP FOR MANY PEOPLE AT ONCE IF YOU PROPOSE A BETTER RULE (#43).

21

AND CARING FOR OTHERS CAN BE AS SIMPLE AS BEING A SITTER (#21) FOR A LITTLE KID.

46

HEAL A BROKEN BOND

Let's say you go out one day and fall down the stairs. Boom—broken arm. That's bad enough. But what if your body couldn't heal? What if your broken arm was like that for the *rest of your life*?

Luckily, our bodies heal. And what's even crazier is that after healing, bones actually become stronger than they were *before* the break.

But here's something most people don't understand: the same is often true of friendships. If a friendship breaks, you don't just have to say, *Well, that's it then—it's broken forever*. You wouldn't ever say that about a broken bone. Just like you might need a cast on your arm, a friendship might need a little help to get back into shape. But it can come back even stronger.

This challenge is about being that help—supporting someone as they repair a friendship, because good friendships are one of the best things in life. Honestly, most people would rather lose an arm than lose their friends. So helping someone fix a friendship? That's a pretty amazing gift.

GETTING STARTED

1 **Talk it through.** Ask both people involved to tell you what happened, privately. You may want to take some notes, both to help you understand and to show them you're taking it seriously.

2 **Separate out the parts.** In those private conversations, you could help each person sort out the situation into parts, like these:

- **Facts:** What a video camera would see. (*The facts are* _____.) Keep these emotion-free, since a video camera couldn't see those.

- **Emotions:** How they felt. (*I felt* _____.)

- **Stories:** What they *thought* was going on—the guesses or assumptions in their head. (*The story I made up is* _____.) This helps separate what *actually* happened from what they *felt* and *believed*.

3 **Start the talk.** Here's where the magic happens. Your goal is a calm, honest conversation. They don't have to agree or apologize—they just have to *listen*. You can pick one person to go first and share their facts, emotions, and stories. The other person repeats back what they heard in their own words, and then they switch roles. After both people have spoken and been heard, ask if either has a request— something they'd like going forward. For example: *I want to feel I can trust you with my stuff* or *I'd like a heads-up if you're upset with me.*

4 **Give it time.** Like a broken bone, hurt feelings don't heal overnight. But if you've helped lead an honest, respectful talk, you've started the healing. If both people are willing, chances are good that the friendship will grow back stronger.

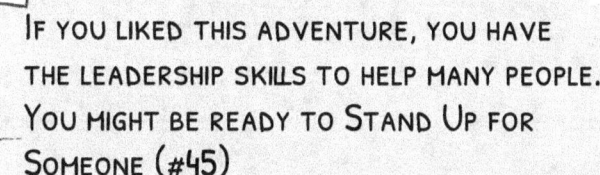

45

IF YOU LIKED THIS ADVENTURE, YOU HAVE THE LEADERSHIP SKILLS TO HELP MANY PEOPLE. YOU MIGHT BE READY TO STAND UP FOR SOMEONE (#45)

39

OR TAKE ON THE CHALLENGE OF STICKING OUT IN A GROUP (#39).

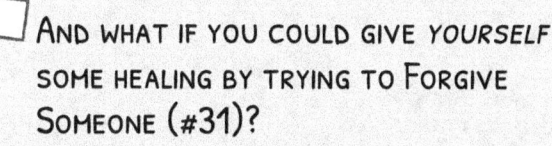

31

AND WHAT IF YOU COULD GIVE *YOURSELF* SOME HEALING BY TRYING TO FORGIVE SOMEONE (#31)?

47
TURN CASH INTO CHANGE

Money has power. Is it good or bad power? Well, that's up to you.

You can earn money, and you can also *raise* money. Raising money means gathering up donations and giving them to a good cause. In case that sounds like a stretch, middle schoolers raise money all the time— they've provided food for the hungry, donated to cancer research, helped build houses, and even saved huge areas of the rainforest from being chopped down.

Raising money for something you believe in might be one of the most satisfying things you can do with money. Not only will it make people's lives better, but working toward a cause is also one of the most meaningful ways to spend time with friends.

GETTING STARTED

1 **What's your cause?** Maybe there's already an issue or need in the world that you want to work on. Great if so! It's also OK if you're not sure yet. If that's the case, ask yourself what issues in the world seem important to you? These might be problems you see in your area, or hear about in the news, or learn about in school. For example, you might be inspired by the idea of building houses for people who don't have one or donating to clean up polluted parts of the Earth.

2 **Make it fun.** There are so many ways to raise money. You could do a bake sale or car wash. You could organize a jogathon, walkathon, or readathon, where people donate for every lap jogged, mile walked, or page read. You could arrange a party, movie night, trivia contest, or talent show, and sell tickets which raise money. You could *crowdfund* the money, which means telling the story of the cause you care about online, and gathering money on a fundraising website.

3 **Teamwork makes the dream work.** You can definitely raise money on your own. But usually it's more fun — and you'll raise more—if friends work with you. Together you'll reach more people, and they'll be inspired that a team of middle schoolers is making this happen.

4 **Promote.** You can get the word out by telling friends, posting signs, making an announcement at school, sending emails, or sharing online (with your family helping you if needed). It helps to have a specific goal of how much money you want to raise and by what day. And here's the good news: when people are really passionate about a cause *and* having a good time, word spreads.

5 **Celebrate.** Whether you raise $10 or $10,000, you've done an amazingly good thing. Actually more than one. You've brought people together around a cause. You've helped take care of people, animals, or the planet in some way. And you've tapped into the positive power of money. Not bad!

18

IF YOU LIKED THIS ADVENTURE, YOU MIGHT WANT TO RAISE MONEY THE OLD-FASHIONED WAY BY ORGANIZING A YARD SALE (#18).

43

IF IT'S THE POWER TO CREATE CHANGE THAT APPEALS TO YOU, IT COULD BE TIME TO PROPOSE A BETTER RULE (#43).

48

RESCUE AN ANIMAL

How often do you get to save a life?

Rescuing an animal might be one of the most meaningful things you ever do. It might lead to a new pet who becomes one of your closest friends, or it might be an animal you only see for a short time, but who will mean a lot to you (and you to them!). It shows you how much you can do for another living being. It's almost guaranteed to be an unforgettable experience.

There are many ways to begin. All of them will require you to get some approval and help from your family, so make sure to talk with them first and get their support. If they don't fully trust you with the responsibility yet, you can ask them what you could do to show you're ready. Maybe they're just a little behind in how capable and responsible you are and need to be reminded that you can handle this!

GETTING STARTED

1 **Support wildlife around you.** You could help local birds by putting up a birdfeeder or help neighborhood critters by making a small garden with plants they can munch on. You could convince your family or whoever manages your building to use fewer pesticides outside. (Pesticides are chemicals that kill unwanted pests, like insects, but some also harm local wildlife).

2 **Start a school club.** You could gather friends who love animals and start a club at school. Together you could raise money for shelters, offer pet-sitting services, and educate others about animal issues.

3 **Volunteer.** There may be an animal shelter or wildlife preserve near you, and often they're happy to have help from volunteers. If you can't yet volunteer, you can show up to their events or help get the word out about their services.

4 **Foster an animal.** Fostering means temporarily caring for an animal until it's adopted by a family. You could check with animal shelters in your area to see if they need foster homes.

5 **Adopt a pet.** This is a big decision, and it depends a lot on what your family is open to, and factors like how much space you have and if anyone is allergic. But if everyone is open to it, this might be a life-changing opportunity. By adopting a pet from a shelter rather than a breeder, you could be saving a life, or at least making a life much, much better! You may want to ask for advice from friends who already have pets, or ask your local animal shelter how to get ready to adopt.

21

IF YOU LIKED THIS ADVENTURE, YOU MIGHT BE INTERESTED IN CARING FOR SOME HUMAN-SHAPED ANIMALS BY BECOMING A SITTER (#21).

47

OR MAYBE YOU'RE FIRED UP TO HELP MORE ANIMALS BY TURNING CASH INTO CHANGE (#47).

16

AND WHAT IF YOU COULD FEEL THE AWE OF SEEING A COLORFUL BIRD ZIP BY YOU — THAT JUST MIGHT HAPPEN TO YOU BY FINDING AWE IN NATURE (#16).

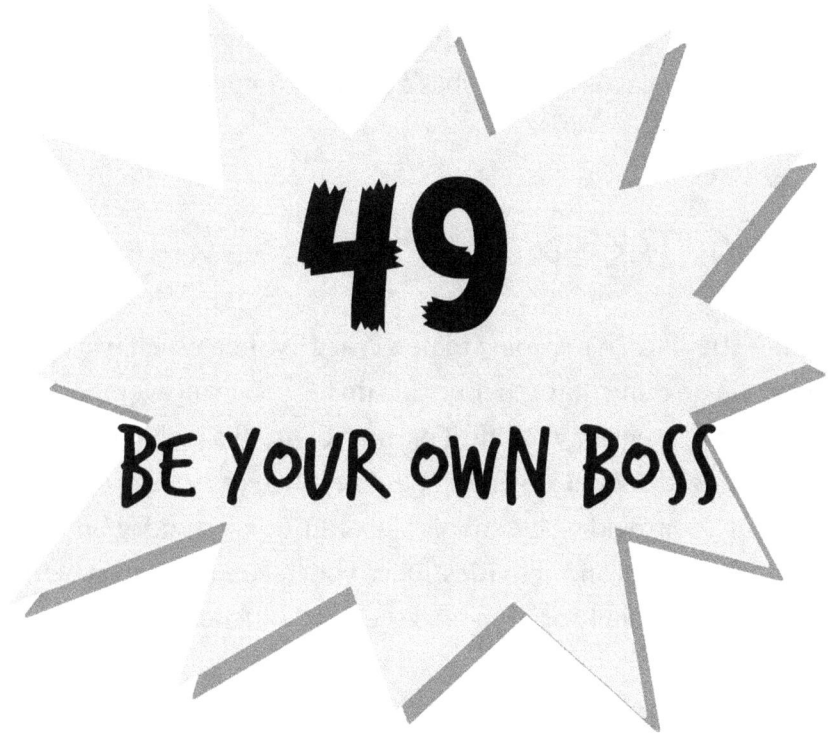

49

BE YOUR OWN BOSS

This one might *sound* easy. If so, you are most likely fooling yourself. It's not easy. Probably somewhere closer to shockingly hard.

If you're interested anyway, here's the challenge. Could you show your family, your friends, and most importantly *yourself* that you have what it takes to live independently for one weekend or even a week? That means buying all the food you need. Cooking it. Cleaning up after yourself. Doing your own laundry. Even (if possible) getting yourself to and from school or anywhere else you need to go.

Why would this possibly be worth doing? Living independently shows people what you can do, and let's be honest—most adults underestimate middle schoolers. Not only will you feel more confident, seeing that you can do hard things well, but you'll prove to others that you can handle more responsibility than they thought. That just might start changing the rules about what's possible for you.

GETTING STARTED

1 **Make the list.** This is going to be a crazy list, because it will contain every single thing that other people do for you in an average weekend or week of your life. For most of us, this is going to be pretty long. It should include things like buying food, cooking it, cleaning up, providing essentials like soap, doing laundry, and getting to school and activities. Once you have a starter list, you can run it by your family or friends so they can add more to it.

2 **Create a budget.** Some of these things might cost money. You could discuss this with your family and see if they would be willing to give you the amount they normally spend on this.

3 **Advice.** Before you start, it would be wise to talk with an adult you trust (probably one of your family members) to make sure that your plans are safe, see if you forgot anything, and think about practicing any skills you might need (like cooking) before you go for it. It's ok to not know how to do all these things. That's why it's a challenge!

4 **Go for it.** Now it's game time. All new skills take practice before you get to be good at them, and this challenge involves several new skills. So if you mess up and have to ask for help, it's all good. This challenge is meant to help you reach a new level, not to be perfect.

5 **Celebrate!** However far you made it, make sure you find a way to celebrate. If you complete the whole weekend or week, you could plan something ahead of time with your family to celebrate your accomplishment. You deserve some applause for this!

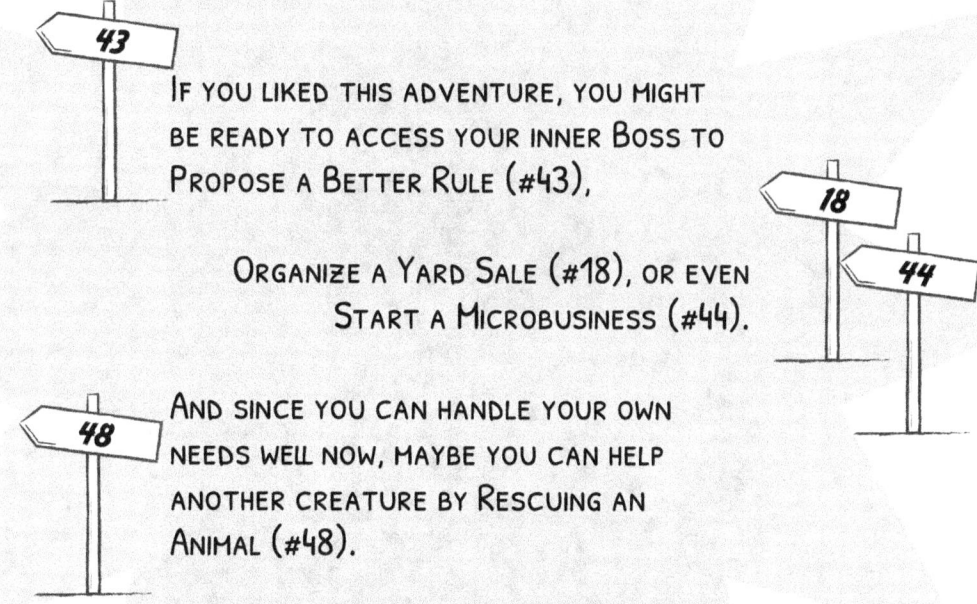

43

IF YOU LIKED THIS ADVENTURE, YOU MIGHT
BE READY TO ACCESS YOUR INNER BOSS TO
PROPOSE A BETTER RULE (#43),

18

44

ORGANIZE A YARD SALE (#18), OR EVEN
START A MICROBUSINESS (#44).

48

AND SINCE YOU CAN HANDLE YOUR OWN
NEEDS WELL NOW, MAYBE YOU CAN HELP
ANOTHER CREATURE BY RESCUING AN
ANIMAL (#48).

50

CREATE YOUR OWN CHALLENGE

There's one *tiny* problem with this book. The whole time it's been suggesting different adventures for you — which are hopefully awesome. But that shouldn't get in the way of *you* creating your own adventure. After all, you know yourself better than anyone.

Have you found yourself wishing for a certain kind of adventure in this book but didn't find it? Or thought you could take one of these adventures *much* further?

Well, if you needed any encouragement, here it is: a blank challenge to be written by you. Every other chapter is for you, but this one is also *by* you. How do you want to challenge yourself?

You know how it goes by now. The goal is not to do something easy. You would have done that already if it mattered to you. The goal is to do something that pushes you out of your comfort zone or stretches what you think are your limits. Something you believe you could do, but you still would be amazed, proud,and maybe even shocked if you actually did it. Now's your chance. What challenge would you create for yourself?

Challenge Name

Why is it worth doing?

Step 1

Step 2

Step 3

!?!

SECRET LAST CHAPTER

Confession: I did *not* like middle school. In fact, I kind of hated it.

Every morning when my alarm went off, I glared at those little red numbers on the clock. It was *way* too early. Positively rude to be woken up at this hour. And especially to have to go to school.

I got so used to disliking school that I almost started thinking that I didn't like learning, since school and learning seemed like more or less the same thing.

But then something changed. Maybe the first change was when I started to keep a journal. I wrote down everything in there—who I had a crush on, ideas for the future, my random thoughts—anything and everything that came to mind. Then I started *doing* things. I got my first job and began to earn some money. That felt *great*. I opened a bank account. I found a mentor. I got so into one of my hobbies that I even went to events at a nearby college to learn more. And those crazy plans and weird hobbies helped me meet some of the best friends I had ever made.

While all this was happening, my hours in school were still pretty crummy. I still did not like waking up that early in the morning. But I realized that school and learning are *not* the same thing. I could create my own adventures. Do my own thing. And not alone, but with friends I found along the way.

That's why I wrote this book. For you to maybe, possibly, in a tiny or big way, realize that you can be in charge of your own learning. Even if middle school isn't great. Even if the adults don't always get it.

You're holding in your hands a set of tickets to all kinds of adventures. My hope is that you'll use them in ways that surprise you—and maybe surprise the people around you, too.

I know this is cheesy, but it's true:

> *You can do anything.*
> *You can go anywhere.*
> *You can be anyone.*

I'll see you out there.

—CHRIS

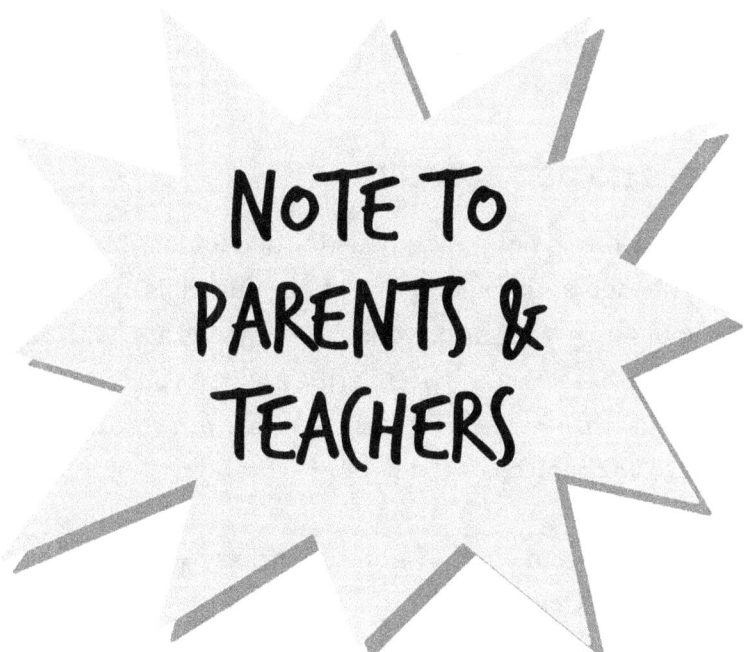

NOTE TO PARENTS & TEACHERS

You are a lucky human. You have one of the most extraordinary jobs that exist—the chance to accompany a young person who is in transformation. Someone bursting with new insights, ideas, and understanding. No pressure!

I know how intense the questions and fears can be along this path. *Will they find truly good friends? When will their current obsession or identity experiment finally be done? Why won't they tell me more about what's happening at school? Are they going to be OK??*

For more than 20 years, I've had the honor of grappling with questions like these, as a middle school teacher, principal, school founder, and dad of a middle schooler. Exploring topics like what does it mean to raise wise, loving, and capable adolescents has transformed me, wrung me out, and created some of the most awe-filled moments of my life. So while this book is 99% for middle schoolers themselves, I have three suggestions for the adults who get to walk alongside them.

❶ There is no perfect adult.

Trying to be perfect is not only exhausting and impossible, but exactly *not* what is needed at this age. Trying to be yourself is more than enough—yourself in the weird, wonderful ways we are, with all our quirks, hobbies, passions, and peculiarities. When you openly share your authentic self, middle schoolers can relax. You've given them permission to be themselves too.

You can't force this, but you can let those masks we adults think we have to wear—the *Don't worry, I'm normal* or *I've got this under control* ones—gradually drop away. Maybe you could fool a younger kid, but middle schoolers are too smart to buy it.

As you show more of who you are, you normalize that humans are complex, emotional, and ever-changing. What a relief that is for everyone, but especially middle schoolers, to accept that about ourselves. Showing more of yourself also means you can show your tools. A middle schooler doesn't want to hear a lecture, but they *are* watching closely. How do you care for a friend who is struggling? How do you celebrate something? How do you recover from a hard day at work? The more you reveal, the more they can learn what it means to be a human in the bigger world they can now perceive.

❷ It's time for a new job description.

Middle schoolers are changing unbelievably quickly. In fact, their rate of brain growth is the fastest it will be for the rest of their lives. Because they're getting smarter by the day, we can't treat them like younger kids. It works better to treat them like something else. My suggestion is to treat them like *heroes*.

Why? Because a middle schooler is a person on a heroic adventure, transforming in both exciting and terrifying ways, making discoveries about themselves, their friends, and the world every day.

If you were on an epic adventure through the wilderness, and could have some help, would you hire a boss to come with you and manage your progress? I wouldn't either. You would probably want to hire a guide. Someone with the authority that comes from experience, but also who would walk alongside you, marvel at the landscape with you, and only intervene if you're about to walk off a cliff.

Imagine that ideal wilderness guide in your mind. That's you now. However you would define that ideal companion, chances are that's the job description for a parent or teacher of a middle schooler.

➌ Since you can't beat 'em, join 'em.

You can't manage a middle schooler's life and growth, at least not without them becoming resentful and resistant sooner or later. But you *can* go on the adventure with them. You can get curious about who they're becoming. You can keep an open mind about their identity experiments, which are developmentally right on track. You can explore some new identities yourself, like picking up that guitar you've always wanted to play, and let them see you in beginner mode, messing up and trying again.

This is the real gift of accompanying a middle schooler through transformation. *You transform too.*

There's one last thing to know about this book.

It may appear to be a bunch of fun side projects—and I hope they truly are fun. But if I had my wish, these challenges would be as important as academics. They would form the core of the real middle school curriculum. The stuff that matters. That helps you figure out who you are and what you can contribute to the world. That turns a wild, tumbling time of life into an adventure worth remembering.

ACKNOWLEDGMENTS

A good day is when I remember that life is an adventure. Not the kind that's fun every second, but the kind that generates meaning and surprise—even magic.

The fact that I can often see life that way is thanks to the adventurous people on the trail with me. I am lucky to know more than I can name here, but to highlight a few: my longtime mentor Michael Mervosh, the always-adventurous Blake Boles, the tireless optimist Tomoko Kusamoto, and the team that joined me in the epic journey of founding Millennium School, including Ann Wang, Ashley Nickels, Jeff Snipes, Lindsay Berk, Michael Fisher, Newton Martin, and Stephen Lessard.

This book is dedicated to my oldest child, Abigail, who was entering her own adventurous middle school years at the time of writing, and who brought the fierce wisdom of that age to help me edit the book. She's served as my teacher in more ways than she can know.

There is a special band of adventurers that I get to facilitate through Argonaut, a community of online advisory groups, and I'd like to honor their help in refining these challenges through countless rounds of practice and feedback. These include Aaron Klein, Adelina Naranjo, Aidyn S, Amara Camacho, Anelle Boone, Aoife Boone, Cameron B, Chase Pinckney, Derya Eransen Lyon, Elliot Skow, Finn McNulty, Grey Allen, Ilona Arias Guerra, Jake Hopkins, Jesse Hopkins, Kamala Hailey Alfonso Decena, Kennedy Cobb, Lander Camacho, Lauren P, Leo Civitano, Lyda Pinckney, Manuel Nino, Mason S, Nathaniel Skow, Oli Rassi, Oliver Johnson, Tenzin Alona Nagase, Wes Robson and Zack McLeod.

To my exceptional editor, Olson Pook, who had a twinkle in his eye from the start when hearing of this book concept and who has made it more playful at every step of the way.

To the extremely kind souls who supported this project on Kickstarter, with special thanks to Jo Balme and Gordon & Patricia Grannis.

And to the best adventure buddy of my life, the one who models how learning and growth make us alive and bring us closer: my wife Misa.